FIXING SIGNS

TWO CURMUDGEONS PET PEEVES

DR. JACK RUNNINGER
&
JUDGE DAN WINN

Copyright © 2010 Dr. Jack Runninger & Judge Dan Winn
All rights reserved.

ISBN: 1451553714
ISBN-13: 9781451553710

EDITOR'S NOTE

One of the few advantages of old age is the privilege of becoming crotchety and cantankerous. This book is a discussion by two curmudgeons of their resultant pet peeves.

It is essentially two books in one. The first section was written by retired Judge Dan Winn. With his keen and perceptive legal mind and experience, he analyzes the things that have gone wrong in our modern society, and what should be done to correct them.

The second part was written by Humorist Jack Runninger, who has received many state and national awards for his newspaper and magazine humor columns. His approach is on seeking the humor and satire in the crazy and aggravating things that people do.

FOREWORD

The philosophy of this book is to demonstrate some thoughtful principles:

1. Genius has its limits, not so with stupidity.

2. A little stupidity can go a long way.

3. The world is much like a good fruitcake---it would not be the same without lots of nuts.

Keep in mind in reading this book, that common sense is not at all common.

Dan Winn
Jack Runninger

TABLE OF CONTENTS

WINN SECTION 1
Health 3
Smokers 3
Body Piercing 4
Snack Foods 5
Restaurants-Restrooms 6
Men's Urinals 6
Mike Royko 7
Criminal And Almost Criminal 9
Imposters Of War 9
Charitable Contributions 12
Irritating Money Vultures 15
Corporate Executive Greed 18
Abby (Abbigail Van Buren) 23
Baseball-Balls & Strikes 27
Tobacco Chewing Ballplayers 28
Weddings 29
Wedding Invitations 32
Ostentation & Affluence 33
You Know 35
YouAll 35
"yes" Telephone 37
Bath Fixtures 39
Thermostats 39
Watch Craze 40
Opulence 40
Light Bulbs 40
Baseball Caps 40
Wasted Talents 41
Bed Making –Hotels & Motels 42

Thoughtless Weather Comments 43
Illegible Signatures 43
Gluttons (contests) 44
Maltreatment of Women 47
False Advertising 49
Overpriced Mail Order..51
Free Gift (Oxymoron) 51
Silly Advertising 52
Prescription Drug Ads...52
Thoughtless Salesperson...53
Grocery Shoppers..53
Blank Check in Mail 55
Surveys (Money Raisers)..55
Magazines 55
Sympathy Notes 55
RSVP..56
Roundabouts 59
Capital Punishment 61
Speeding Laws 62
Driving While Drinking 63
Courts..64
Driver –Intersection Hesitation...64
Just Preposterous...65

RUNNINGER SECTION 67
Introduction..69
Folks Who Talk Too Much..70
Folks Who Talk Too Little 71
Gloomy People..71
Pessimists...72
Toilet Seats...73
People Who Don't Use Deodorant....................................74
Braggarts..74
Prolonging Boring Speakers With Inane Questions...........75
Boring Long Windedspeakers..76
People Who Won't Admit They're Wrong........................77
Rude Parkers 79
Idiot Drivers 80
People Who Can Remember Names.................................81
Mr. Gunderson 84
My Wife's First Husband 85
People Who Resent Preacher Jokes 86
Tv Evangelists...88
Difficult Cab Drivers..89
Gullible Folks..90
Those Who Feed On The Gullible 92
Looking Foolish...93
Double Last Names..95
Phoning The Doctor 97
Smartasses..100
Stupidity...100
People Who Think I'm Stupid 101
People Who Think Rednecks Are Stupid........................104
Verbiage Showoffs 106
Unsolicitous Solicitors..108
Cheapskates..110
Doctors Who Make Me Wait 111

Complainers	112
Confusing Religion With Magic	112
Selfish Religion And Charity	114
My Time Is Your Time?	116
Organ Recitals	116
Tv Remotes	117
A Night Out	117
Dishonesty	117
Phone Nuisances	119
Business Buzz Words	119
Showoff Athletes	119
Insects	120
Useless And Maddening Words	120
Inappropriate Cursing	121
Boasting About Getting Drunk	121
Household Paraphernalia	121
A Sweet Wife	122
Barbecue Signs	122
Rate Increases	123
Wives' Answers	123
Dogs	124
Lassie Tv Program	125
Dogs Hurt My Reputation	126
Cutesy Grandparent Names	128
People Who Give Bad Advice	129
My Lousy Memory	130
Loud Kids	131
Male Chauvinism	132
Wives' Imperfections	133
Martyrs	134
Wife Inefficiency	135
Women's House Décor	137
Political Correctness	138

Being A Job Reference	140
Teaching A Wife To Drive	141
Yankee Critics	143
Life Isn't Fair	145
No Sympathy	146
Graduations	148
Observant People	150
Communicating With Kids	151
Not Listening	152
Being A Number	153
Non-Communicative Communication	155
My Investing Stupidity	156
Being A Lousy Entrepreneur	158
Quick Thinkers	160
Understanding English Language	162
People Who Are Too Agreeable	164
People Who Don't Show Appreciation	165
I Ain't As Purty As I Used To Be	165
Getting Confused More Easily	167
Can't Do Things I Used To	167
Lame Excuses	168
Profundities	170
Things That Are "Good For You"	172
Being A War Hero	174
Christmas Newsletters	175
Female Memories	176
Female Logic	177
De-Personalized Service	178
Poor Service	179
Impolite Folks	181
Those Who Are Always Right	182
Self-Importance	182
Swifties	183

Christmas Toy Assembly	184
Censorship	186
Being A Lousy Football Player	187
Lousy At Basketball Too	189
Mondegreens	190
Standing In Line	192
The GPS Lady	194
Computers	195
Irish Bulls	196
Cajun Stories	197
Puns	199
Senior Tennis	200
Being A Lousy Golfer	202
Legal Oddities	203
Snakes	205
Women Who Think Men Insensitive	206
Practical Jokes	208
Flying	210
The Lottery	212
Treating Seniors With Condescension	212
Littering	214
Seeking Perfection	214
Efficiency Experts	217

WINN SECTION

Pet peeves and irritants are also interesting, amusing, and we also have the fond hope that writing about them might have a positive effect and change some conduct for the better.

These quirks and oddities and just bad conduct are in categories which may help the reader appreciate them.

HEALTH

SMOKERS

Smoking is first in this chapter of the book as it is not only one of the more deadly of all the irritants in the world but it is also one of the most expensive of all irritants in the world. The effects of smoking on the health of the population is well known and should not need any repeating; however, a few of the salient points concerning smoking should be made here.

Each year 400,000 Americans die from cigarette smoking. One-third of the 3,000 home fire deaths is from smoking. 8,600,000 Americans suffer from smoke related chronic disease. Lost productivity from smoking costs the U.S. $92,000,000,000 in lost productivity.

In addition to the deadly and costly nature of smoking and smokers, they can be the most inconsiderate of all people. They do not think that cigarettes are trash, dumping them wherever they end their smoking, on immaculate floors, on wooden floors that can be damaged and most idiotic of all is the dumping of them in toilets and urinals, where there is no drain for them to exit.

Smokers do not acknowledge that second hand smoke is of any consequence to anyone else and think that their smoking is a basic constitutional human right no matter how it affects anyone in their vicinity. Of course they rationalize by pointing out some ninety year old person that still smokes and they point out that their physical was passed with flying colors and there is no need to quit smoking.

New research shows that smokers outside businesses, bars and restaurants are a positive health hazard to nonsmokers. The level of continine, a nicotine byproduct used as an indicator of tobacco exposure, was double in nonsmokers outside restaurants and 162% higher outside bars.

We must acknowledge that so far as they are concerned it is useless and really counterproductive to quit before you have lung cancer or emphysema.

Does the health risk, higher Medicare costs, higher medical costs, higher insurance costs, more sickness and earlier death to our loved ones irritate you constantly? It should.

Though not for smokers alone, a great sign on smoking was on a church sign: "Where will you spend eternity—in smoking or non-smoking?"

BODY PIERCING

Piercing of ears, so standard for women (and men in recent years) has now proliferated into a fad of piercing the eyelids, nose, belly-button and even the tongue. This irritant to view is also a dangerous and unhealthy practice.

While tongue piercing is repulsive to view and medically dangerous, the person may not be dumber than an ox; but as James Thurber said "—he is not any smarter."

SNACK FOODS

This author very much likes Coca-Cola and would probably enjoy one regularly and too often. Nothing wrong with the Coca-Cola being a way of life in the South and elsewhere in the world.

However, if children are in the habit of having to have a soft drink and a snack many times during the day, it is not only a bad habit but is bad for their health; and incidentally it is costly.

It seems that whenever most children are near any food store or place where food is sold they have to have something to drink or eat and the time of time seems irrelevant. Late in the evening or before meals is just as apt to be a time they want soft drinks or snacks and this is bad for their health (and expensive).

They also seem to need chewing gum regularly and of all the things which seem to be demanded by the younger generation, chewing gum is one of the most prevalent of all snack type foods.

If children could realize from their youth the unusual waste of having to have something in their mouths a greater portion of the day, they would be far better off financially, and with their health.

It is a way of life for a great portion of the populace to either have to chew gum, eat snacks to pacify some perceived hunger, or drink some soft drink to pacify some imagined thirst. This way of life has become very costly to many families who could use the money much better otherwise and any obesity is certainly a proper concern for youth, and for any individual overweight adult. There is no federal or governmental regulation that could help on this. It can be reversed by knowledge and education on food and drink.

RESTAURANTS-RESTROOMS

Health authorities bombard us with instructions to keep our hands clean as they are a major carrier of germs.

Yet restaurants, clubs and most businesses continue to have restrooms with doors opening "in" requiring a pull on a door handle (unsanitary). Particularly thoughtless for eating establishments.

Can you think of a more frequent irritant in a restaurant than someone coming to your table (friend or foe) and wanting to shake hands with you as you are trying to eat? Or coming to the table and talking right over the table; spewing saliva.

MEN'S URINALS

Nothing in the building world is more senseless or stupid or irritating than the design of urinals in men's restrooms.

These everywhere have not been changed in design in modern times from a design from which promotes wetting the floor around the urinal and with the millions of urinals about the country and the many companies who make these fixtures it is appalling that the design has never been corrected.

MIKE ROYKO

This chapter will quote from some other people who have irritants. Mike Royko, a columnist for the Chicago Tribune, had a number of what he called "gripes". Some of them:

(1) He says "Men that say 'We're pregnant'". He challenges "We're pregnant" by 'hardly true'; only one is pregnant.

(2) "Dumb newscaster and traffic reporters who say 'left hand side of the street, right hand turn, left hand shelf'." "What on earth does your hand have to do with it?"

(3) "Working women who say to a homemaker 'What in the world do you do all day?'"

(4) "Parents who have been unable and unwilling to make honorable citizens of their offspring, and when caught, claim that the system has failed them."

(5) "Schools giving out free condoms to students. Why? Are they planning to have sex in class?"

CRIMINAL AND ALMOST CRIMINAL

IMPOSTERS OF WAR

For those who have served honorably in the military, and also patriotic Americans the more nauseating class of people are those who claim to be war heroes and recipients of metals that they did not earn and are called "Rambo wannabees". For some years now the FBI has been diligently pursuing people who claim to have been in the war and who masquerade as war heroes.

Most all medals are easily obtainable at military bases and military stores, that is, all except the Medal of Honor which would be quite hard to obtain.

A good illustration of one who wore all of the top medals including the Bronze Star, the Silver Star and the Navy Cross, (the Navy Cross being second in rank only to the Medal of Honor), is a man named Gerard Smigel. He masqueraded as a war hero and attended a Marine Corp. birthday ball near Atlantic City in a quite dramatic dress blue uniform and as the rank of a Lieutenant Colonel.

Smigel gave himself away to a Marine who attended the birthday ball by referring to several things which did not fit the Marine jargon, particularly saying that he was going to the "latrine". When in fact, Marines and the Navy call it the "head". After being thus caught, Smigel pleaded guilty in Federal Court to illegally wearing the uniform and medals and was sentenced to three years probation and a fine of $3,000.00. (Quite a lenient sentence).

Wes Cooley, a former representative from Oregon, claimed to have served with the Army Special Forces in Korea when actually he only served stateside. He was sentenced to pay a fine of $7,000.00 and ordered to perform 100 hours of community service after being convicted in 1997 of lying on official documents.

Patrick Couwenberg, a Los Angeles Superior Court Judge claimed to have served in Vietnam as an Army Corporal and received a Purple Heart for being wounded, and a man that worked as a CIA operative in Laos in the 1960's, when he actually was only in the US Naval Reserves stateside from 1965 to 1969. He was removed from the bench by the California Commission on Judicial Performance on August 15, 2001 for willful misconduct in office and conduct prejudicial to the administration of justice and improper action under the state constitution.

Michael O'Brien, a former Kane County, Illinois Judge claimed to have received the Medal of Honor as a sailor for action off Lebanon in 1958, when in fact no Medals of Honor were awarded during the 1958 Lebanon Campaign and Navy personnel did not engage in combat there. He was exposed when he applied for the Medal of Honor license plate in 1992 and resigned from the bench on December 4, 1995.

Donald Nicholson, Chief of Amelia, Ohio Police Department from 1982 to 1986 claimed to have served four tours of duty in Vietnam with the Army and while serving with the Fifth Special Forces on February 1, 1970 was captured and held for fifteen days as a POW, earning him the Distinguished Service Cross. Actually his service in the Navy was from 1964 to 1968 but never in Vietnam. He admitted in 1999 that he had purchased the Distinguished Service Cross and forged documents for $2,000.00 in order to gain increase Veteran's Administration benefits and was sentenced to three years of probation and a fine of $300.00 on August 10, 2000.

The last of the illustrations that I will give for this 'low life' irritating (criminal) group is that of history professor, Joseph Ellis of Mount Holyoke College in Massachusetts. The delightful professor had won a Pulitzer Prize and a national book award and was given credit for providing students with a realistic view of war through his tales of combat in Vietnam.

He endeared himself to the academics by claiming to have transformed himself into an anti-war protestor after returning home from duty as a paratrooper and platoon leader.

While Ellis did serve in the Army, he was enrolled in graduate school at Yale from 1965 through 1969. His three years of active duty from 1969 to 1972 were spent teaching history at West Point. When confronted with this sorry conduct, Ellis made the most repulsive halfway apology one could imagine. "Even in the best of lives mistakes are made, I deeply regret having let stand and later confirming the assumption that I went to Vietnam. For this and any other distortions about my personal life I want to apologize to my family, friends, colleagues and students. Beyond that circle however, I shall have no further comment." How disgustingly arrogant is this statement which thumbs his nose at genuine Vietnam War veterans who were directly insulted with his pathetic fabrications and how insulting not to apologize to all veterans and to his State and Nation for his repulsive conduct.

This list is to give the reader an idea of how these imposters act. These are only a minute group of hundreds or thousands who have dishonored service to our country by insulting the memories of those who patriotically served and died for our nation.

Any wonder this is the top <u>irritant</u> in the world for all veterans and probably many patriots.

CHARITABLE CONTRIBUTIONS

Charitable contributions and all of the various aspects of charitable giving should be right at the top of the list of all irritants to every taxpayer. Tax deductions for charitable giving have always been a great source of irritation. It has always seemed that it should be unconstitutional to have tax deductions for charitable contributions to charities, to funds, to societies even though all do good work.

Why is this an irritant and why is it wrong in many respects? Well, it just does not seem right for someone in church to give $100,000.00 as a tax deductible gift and the federal government in effect pays about $33,000.00 of that. (Query: if the federal Treasury loses that amount, is it the same as paying?) Whereas, if a person at my church gives $1,000.00 to their church, the federal government is only paying $300 of that.

A gimmick in the tax code allows giving appreciated stock or property to a charity, receive a tax deduction, and no tax paid to the government. The tax ramifications of charitable giving are really endless. All good charitable groups now try to get you to participate in a long term scheme to do the government out of taxes and promote charitable contributions to be devised in such a way as to prevent its being taxed.

Giving to a church or giving to the American Cancer Society or American Heart Association should not be done for tax purposes but should be done out of the goodness of my heart.

It is doubtful that we will have drastic tax reform but should the 'fair tax' be implemented it would do away with these awful tax deductible schemes which are designed to keep money from the federal treasury that should otherwise logically go there. Of course, charitable foundations have done tremendous good. But the flip side of this allows a billionaire to put a billion dollars into a foundation as opposed to being taxed on it, he is using, in effect, a large amount of what would otherwise be taxable funds in his charitable pursuits. Even though they are admirable. Billions of dollars are diverted from the U.S. Treasury in this manner.

A great flaw in the charitable contribution deduction for tax purposes is that the fund has no obligation to spend a substantial amount on the cause for which the donor contributed. Many charitable funds pay more for fund raising and for its employees and officials than is paid for the purposes of the charity. Some even pay only a small percentage of the income of the charitable fund toward the object of the charity, sometimes 10% or below. There is also no control over the sometimes exorbitant pay for the officers of the fund and there is no control over the pay for a rogue minister who uses the church as a bank for his unbelievable extravagant lifestyle, multi-million dollar mansion and multi-million dollar lifestyle.

One rogue fund raising minister recently gave $1,000,000 to a school of his choice.

A typical practice for officials in many charitable organizations is to award large bonuses even though they are not related to performance. Similar to the corporate excesses mentioned elsewhere in this book. There certainly should be an enforceable criteria for denying the charitable status of a church wherein most of the income goes to a multi-million dollar lifestyle for the pastor. Likewise, there should be a control method of denying charitable status to a fund or organization which pays out exorbitant amounts of the funds' proceeds to its officials and fundraisers, and for exorbitant expense accounts.

There is no enforcement by Internal Revenue in denying charitable status or eliminating charitable status for monetary abuse by the fund and its officials or by a church and its officials. If the tax code needs to strengthen this enforcement provision it should be done. It would help eliminate this extreme irritant for all taxpayers.

POLITICAL LEADERSHIP FUNDS

Irritating Money Vultures

This chapter is not meant to criticize or comment on fundraising practices of the Republican, Democratic or any other party participating in elections.

It is to point out how bad some political leadership funds are in their greedy solicitation and spending of funds which really harm valid fundraising efforts by Democrats and Republicans and any other valid party fundraisers. Bob Barr, a former U.S. Representative from Georgia is probably the most disgusting of these fundraisers and is a great illustration of what these vultures can do.

On May 18, 2008 the Atlanta Journal Constitution provided great enlightenment on Bob Barr and several other political leadership funds and their distribution of money raised from people conscientiously wanting to participate in the funding of their electoral candidates.

The AJC itemized seven of these funds and analyzed the amount raised against the amount donated and the percentages donated were quite revealing and quite disgusting in three of the funds.

Bob Barr was the most disgusting of the entire group giving only 4% of the percentage donated since January, 2007.

These two worst funds were:

Progressive Patriot Fund-Senator Russ Reingold (D-Wis), raised $1,666,726.00 and donated $144,075.00 –9%

Bob Barr Leadership Fund-Ex. Rep. Bob Barr (R-Ga), raised $1,393,750.00 and donated $51,050.00—4%

The newspaper further analyzed Bob Barr's leadership fund since 2003 and stated that he had raised $4,300,000.00 since 2003 and then in the last five years the fund has given $125,200.00 to federal candidates and another $81,875.00 went to state and local campaigns.

Among the neat little items included in the expenses were $41,109.00 in salary for Barr's son Derek and a $500.00 political consulting fee for his son Adrian. Also, $865.00 travel for Barr's wife Jeri. Having been a Republican Congressman, Barr was appealing to conservative Republicans to defeat liberal Congress candidates and it is enlightening as to how he worded his letters seeking funds. Just listen.

"Today, because the stakes have been raised with Hillary Clinton and Chuck Schumer's massive fundraising advantage, I'm hoping you will lend me a hand by doubling your gift to $180.00

With so many close races predicted in Georgia, New Hampshire, Colorado and Texas, to name just a few, I hope I can count on you as we fight to defend and elect rock-solid conservative leaders.

I've gone ahead and taken the extra step of attaching $0.41……….."

The news report states that Barr claimed his fund played a "tremendous role" in ousting Senator Tom Daschle, a Democrat from South Dakota in 2004 and provided critical funding in 2006 for Freshman Representative Michele Bachman, a Republican from Minnesota. His records show the fund made a very modest donation of $1,000.00 to John Tune, Daschle's opponent and only $1,500.00 to Bachman.

It should probably not shock us at this time that Barr's fund gave $12,000.00 to the Libertarian National Committee that apparently was never even mentioned in any of his letters pleading for funds from conservatives. The reason it is not surprising at this time is that he had diverted his attention from the Republican conservative causes to seeking the nomination of the Libertarian party to run for President.

Author's note: The Libertarian party nominated Barr as their Presidential candidate financing his ego trip around the country along with his family being paid for the next year or at least until the November election. It is almost unbelievable that the Libertarian party would nominate someone as their candidate who raised $1,393,750.00 and only spent 4% on the cause for which he was raising the funds. He would be a great leader, conservative at that.

The Atlanta Journal-Constitution now uses him as an editorial writer. His articles on ethics in fundraising should be classic.

This awful fundraising is quite irritating and harmful in that it makes those who want to contribute to political candidates and parties skeptical of how their donations will be used. Damages the whole political process.

Professional fundraisers, (including irritating telemarketers), we have learned will keep most of the funds raised.

Interesting information is furnished by "Pennies for Charity", which is an annual report on non-profit groups by the New York Attorney General's office. For 2004, the report noted that of $187,000,000 raised by 592 charities only $63,000,000 went to the charities themselves. Only one-third going to the charity is a poor return.

The report of "Pennies for Charity" pointed out one corporation "All-Pro Telemarketing Associates Corporation" raised $4.1 million in 2003 for 15 charities including disabled children, disabled police officers, children with leukemia and a program that helped find missing children. Only 13% or $533,000 went to the charities. What a miserable return and what an irritant.

CORPORATE EXECUTIVE GREED

Anyone with any amount of stock or any knowledge of the business section of newspapers should readily understand this irritant and how executive pay has been really a disgrace to the management of many of the large corporations in the United States. The increase in executive compensation has been almost astronomical compared to the increase in the pay of the average worker in these corporations. No wonder it is an irritant every time the average worker or average American reads about it.

No one can argue that the executives should not be adequately paid well above that of any of the employees; however, when you consider 100% raises in pay for an executive making millions of dollars and compare that to a 3%, 4% or 8% raise for the employees of that corporation there is something drastically wrong and irritating.

The maneuvering to pay executives that are not entitled to huge compensation or huge compensation increases is startling at times. The maneuvering to pay an executive who has been only mediocre and is rewarded with bonuses or huge retirement packages is brought about by, many times, what we could call shenanigans.

This writer noticed exorbitant and unusual executive compensation for a number of years but in a surprising development, while owning AT&T stock some years ago, it was disclosed that the company was reorganizing over a period of time to eliminate 40,000 jobs.

With this master plan to reorganize the AT&T and cut 40,000 employees out of a job, because of the expertise of the CEO of the company, he was awarded several million dollars for his expertise in maneuvering the company into making 40,000 employees lose their jobs.

That did not seem right. What an irritant!

One of the more fortunate times that this writer sold stock at the right time was this occasion. AT&T stock at that time was approximately $60.00 and because of this rather sickening and cruel maneuvering of the finances of the employees and the Chief Executive I sold my stock.

I sold it not thinking it would go down particularly but a consequence of the operation of AT&T made it begin to drop lower and lower and lower and it had to occur to this writer that the employees of AT&T were certainly not impressed with how the management felt about their livelihood and their security, as compared to the management, and it certainly seems logical that the irritation of the employees with the management ruining the lives of many people and saving money for AT&T, to give a bonus to the CEO, could have had something to do with the company going downhill. I do not know.

The illustrations of irritating executive compensation deals are endless. In 2007 Robert Nardelli had $210,000,000 given to him as a departure compensation "gift" and it followed a very unproductive and mediocre stint as head of Home Depot.

It should be noted here in connection with Robert Nardelli who left Home Depot with a severance package of over $200,000,000.00, that during his mediocre performance at Home Depot from 2004, he received an 11.2% raise in 2005. Imagine how irritating to the average employee with some 3% to 4% raise.

Angelo Mozillo, a CEO for Countrywide Financial made $103,000,000 in 2006. This great leader and the directors who looked after his compensation began selling shares after 2006 and the firm lost $19.7 billion dollars in market value in 2007. What great leadership!

It should also be noted about Angelo Mozillo, mentioned previously, that when Bank of America bought Countrywide Financial, which was almost headed for bankruptcy, Mozillo made over $100,000,000.00 in the transaction.

Another good illustration of an irritating CEO raise was Bellsouth Corporation CEO Duane Ackerman, whose 2004 $11,000,000.00 compensation was raised 34% to over $15,000,000.00.

When Boston Scientific lost $500,000,000.00 because of concern with its stints and defibrillators, James R. Toben, the CER, had his pay raised by 29%. Another stunning payout involved Citigroup, whose CEO Charlie Prince, while conducting the company through its massive losses during the subprime debacle in which Citi wrote off some $41,000,000,000.00 the Board awarded Charlie Prince a $10.4 million dollar bonus on top of $28,000,000.00 in stock options.

While non-profit groups will be dealt with in another chapter, we should note here an unusual CEO in Atlanta, Georgia. Fred Bradley, CEO of the Metro Atlanta YMCA, makes $290,000.00 and gets a performance and retention bonus for staying on in the amount of $250,000.00. Whose check really is this?

Another rather startling, greedy CEO payout involved Coca-Cola Enterprises CEO John Brock. The top executives were not paid their bonuses in 2006 for failing performance targets. They announced that they would cut 3,500 employees during the next two years. Probably because of the lack of performance of the company.

While gouging these employees for their jobs, the executives of Coca-Cola Enterprises were given $3.6 million in cash awards. "Award" being a crazy title to allow them to replace the bonuses they had missed for failing to make performance targets.

Nothing is more irritating than for a CEO to be given a bonus while figuring out how to cut and fire loyal employees. Somewhat routine also seems to be the Exxon Mobile Corporation CEO, Rex Tillerson, receiving an 18% raise in 2007. Just standard for the industry.

If the reader wants to know of a more irritating payout for CEOs than any of the above, just listen to the Mirant Corporation in bankruptcy. Here is a company in bankruptcy, losing jobs approximating 4,500 and during bankruptcy gave a severance package of $4.25 million dollars for the former CEO, Marcee Fuller and awarded a severance package of $8.2 million dollars to Michelle Burns, the Chief Financial Officer without any regard for the company and its employees.

Another executive debacle involving a bankrupt corporation was Delta Airlines' CEO Leo Mullin. Mullin had big bonuses given to the top executives in 2002, while in bankruptcy, and explained this by saying that he wanted to keep the management team together. What a great team to lead a company into bankruptcy and then Mullin who was not a long time employee of Delta received a $16,000,000.00 severance when he left the company shortly after that. Even more startling concerning these bonuses was that they were dished out at the time Delta was requesting the federal government to help bail them out and keep them afloat during and after its bankruptcy. There were loud and long screams from members of Congress and the public.

Excessive compensation for executives is not limited to corporations and sadly permeates some federal agencies.

The Veteran's Affairs Departments has awarded bonuses to nearly two dozen officials who also sat on the boards recommending the payments.

All of this while the agency had a budget $1.3 billion dollars short and was jeopardizing veterans' healthcare. 21 of 32 officials who were members of a veteran's administration performance review board received more than half a million dollars in payments. These senior officials had devised a flawed 2005 budget. A bad specific instance involved Michael Walcoff, Associate Deputy Undersecretary, who sits on two of the Review Boards and his wife, Kimberly Walcoff, a VA Director, who received bonuses totaling $42,000.00. The Associated Press reported $3.8 million dollars in bonuses to these officials of the Department of Veteran's Affairs with annual bonuses to the Senior VA officials in 2005 averaging more than $16,000.00. The highest average in government.

Discretionary bonuses in government should not be allowed in any event.

Almost every annual meeting and request for votes by the stockholders of a corporation includes a provision to amend the stockholder equity incentive plan to increase the number of shares available for grants for executive compensation or awards to insiders of the corporation. They further request a change to remove limitations on grants of awards to executives.

ABBY (ABBIGAIL VAN BUREN)

Abby (Abigail Van Buren), in her delightful columns, had a nice collection of her pet peeves, all of them concerning poor or incorrect grammar as follows.

"The 'lie' and 'lay' confusion: To 'lay' means to set or put—to "lie" means to recline. Remember, chickens lay eggs. People lie down."

"The use of 'all are not' when the person means 'not all are'. Example, saying 'All women are not beautiful,' when one means, 'Not all women are beautiful.' "

"We frequently hear 'between you and I.' Wrong! It's 'between you and me.' Another irritant is 'try and' instead of 'try to.' For example, one may try to win—then lose. But how can one try and win—and then lose?"

"One hears supposedly educated people say 'between she and I' instead of the correct 'between her and me.' "

"And how about the word 'irregardless'? Just plain 'regardless' will do, but regardless of how 'irregardless' grates on one's nerves, it has nosed its way into the dictionary. (It means 'regardless.')"

"Talk about overusing a word, I nominate 'basically.' People who start every other sentence with the word 'basically' usually have limited vocabularies."

"My pet peeve – double negatives: 'I don't know nothing' and 'he don't go nowhere' are the worst offenders."

"Some people think the plural of "you" is "youse". It's not. "You" is both singular and plural."

"The word "forte" (meaning strong point) is pronounced "fort" – not "for-tay"!"

"Also, people use the word "snuck" instead of "sneaked" Although "snuck" somehow sneaked into the dictionary, it's not used by people who use proper English."

"Ask someone to define "hoi Polloi" and it's a good bet that he will say "high-tone or upper class." Actually it means "the masses" – or the general population."

"Nuclear" is pronounced "nuke-lee-er" –not "nuke-you-ler"!

"And how about "he's got," "she's got and "they've got? The correct word is "has." ("He has," "she has"…."got" has got to go!)"

"The month of February has two "R's" in it –but we keep hearing "Feb-yoo-ary."

"We frequently hear that a man has "prostrate" trouble, when he actually has "pros-TATE" trouble."

"Another error—using the word "myself" instead of "me." Example: "If you have any questions, see Bobby or myself after the meeting." "See Bobby or me" is correct."

"The "infer" and "imply" mix-up: The writer "implies", the reader "infers," (It's like pitching and catching.)"

"Please do not say "o" instead of "zero". Or use the word "that" when "who" is correct. ("That" refers to inanimate objects; "who" to people.)"

"Now, lend me your ear: Don't use "loan" as a verb, as in "Loan me a twenty." It should be, "Lend me a twenty." "Loan" is a noun; "lend" is a verb."

"Finally, the misuse of the word "ask": Some say "ax" instead of "ask." I would much rather be "asked" than "axed." Wouldn't you?"

One of Abby's readers sent in their pet peeve with news media who say "a million and a half dollars" when they mean "one and a half million dollars", pointing out that a "million and a half dollars" can only mean one million dollars and 50 cents. The reader also noted that a news person said the Savings and Loan scandal may cost "a trillion and a half dollars." He offered to pay the 50 cents and make it an even.

SPORTS

BASEBALL

Balls and Strikes

A huge irritant to this author has been the umpiring and calling of balls and strikes in baseball.

There is a defined precise area for home plate which fits each batter and this defined area between the knees and the chest is supposed to be precise.

It can never be precise in leaving it to the split second judgment of an umpire. There are numerous times when the conduct of an umpire in calling balls and strikes is analyzed to show that he is calling them different from the norm; whatever the norm is supposed to be. At times the umpire is said to be calling strikes a little bit high; not dishonestly, but correct in his judgment. The sports analysts say that he is consistent in this, therefore, it is ok since he calls them wrong for both teams.

Frequently, the umpire will be said to call balls on the outside of the plate, not dishonestly, as he calls them for both teams the same.

This same reasoning of course has been used on umpires that call balls too far inside or too low. If would will only think about the huge importance of a ball or a strike in Major League Baseball, the World Series, any important games wherein an inch or two could make the difference in the losing or winning of the World Series, a Pennant, a League or any other critical game and one could consider all of them critical to the players themselves.

The technology exists which could correct this and the lamenting that it would detract from the old line of having the umpire call the balls and strikes could be eliminated by allowing the umpire to call them in the same fashion as they are called now except that he could be electronically perfect as to each batter and each ball and strike as opposed to the huge margin of error in every close ball and strike in any baseball game.

In my irritant about the failure to take advantage of technology in calling balls and strikes in major league baseball particularly; it should be noted that the National Football League has instant replay and there are only some two or three decisions by the referees which are called into question in any given game. The same can be said for professional tennis where instant replays are used when a call is made on the tennis court and the error by the officials is extremely rare and extremely correct most of the time.

TOBACCO CHEWING BALLPLAYERS

What a great spectacle; a ballplayer with his cheek sticking out from a huge chew of tobacco. Great for the sport? Great as a role model? For youth?

FAMILY

WEDDINGS

Very burdensome for the average income family in recent decades has been the cost of weddings. Out of proportion to the income of the family involved. While the sky is the limit seems to be the approach of the wealthy when weddings are involved, the sad state of affairs for the average or below average income family is very sickening.

We have reached the stage where the thought is that we must spend lavishly on the wedding gown, the parties for the bride and decorations and accessories for the wedding itself which must be very lavish in order to satisfy the bride that we have done right by her and her wedding.

Raymond Atkins had a delightful article in the Rome News Tribune in 2007 concerning his daughter's wedding preparations which is all too common, and all too revealing, about the extraordinary cost of weddings.

Atkins describes how he once was invited to go with his wife and daughter to a fancy bridal boutique to arrange for the bridal gown. Atkins described the sales person as a "wedding associate" who immediately inquired as to what the budget was for the bridal gown.

Atkins was feeling extremely generous in regard to his daughter's wedding and stated that he wanted it to be first class and he might go even $500 or $600 if she really liked the gown.

After stunned silence from the sales person, his wife and daughter, Atkins was invited to leave the boutique and allow the wife and daughter to proceed with the purchase of the bridal gown while he waited outside in the car. When the wife and daughter came out some three hours later, they were ecstatic and handed him the receipt for the bridal gown, which he received with tears in his eyes.

Thinking to himself that it was more than he had paid for all but two of the cars he had owned during his forty years of driving, he thought maybe the price included the services of the sales person to paint his house and mow the lawn.

He said the pain of the knowledge of the cost was intensified when he was informed that they still had a fitting fee, shoes, undergarments and a veil to go. While someone such as Raymond Atkins can pay the bill for such wedding preparations, it is all too often that the average family is not able to pay the costs which seem to be demanded and expected by the bride to be. There does not seem to be a logic or anything but selfishness in the preparation of a wedding which will not only cost the family and the bread winner more than is proper within its budget but is many times enough to make a down payment on a home for the couple or to give them a financial start in their wedded life.

Thoughtlessness about the cost to the breadwinner of the family is sometimes not as thoughtless as those who are asked to participate in the wedding. Six bridesmaids are usually required to buy their own matching dresses at $200, $300, $400 and upwards to satisfy the bride's whims. That those bridesmaids will have to struggle, or their families will have to struggle, in order to pay for their dress which is designed by the bride is seldom of concern to the bride. Trying to talk reason to a bride (and her mother) is about like blowing a trumpet from the wrong end.

Of course, we thought we had seen many of the most extravagant costs of weddings, bridal gowns, church decorations, parties and gifts until recent years, when the fashion became to take the whole wedding entourage to an exotic place for the wedding. Someplace like the Bahamas, Bermuda, some resort town 1,000 miles away, even the Mexican Coast for a wedding. This means that the entourage has to go in its entirety, that is, all of the bridesmaids and the men and it requires any number of families to go for the wedding not only in support of the bridesmaids whose families are usually friends of the bride and groom, but it requires that they go and spend some three or four days an at expensive resort to satisfy the whim of the bride to be married in an exotic place with no connection to the family. This author's granddaughter did not get married until she was in her thirties. She was very mature along with the fine man she had agreed to marry. They were both mature and capable of paying for a wedding, which they decided to have some 300 miles away from our home of Cedartown, Georgia, in an exotic location atmosphere. She of course expected her grandfather and all of the immediate family to come there for the wedding so three or four days expense for at least 20 or 30 people. This grandfather said "I am so happy for both of you and I think you will make a good couple and I hope you have a nice wedding 300 miles from here but I will not be there. I will give you a gift for the wedding but I will not come 300 miles to attend a wedding that could just as easily have been held here. Not only for the convenience but for the practical expense of the entire family which would have to attend". Of course the granddaughter was shocked, as was my daughter and some of the other family members. But, after thinking it over, my granddaughter and the man she was going to marry found an old museum-quality home that was available for weddings very near here and had a magnificent wedding. It was as nice and memorable as one could hope for without the foolish draining of funds from themselves and their family in traveling over 300 miles to see the same ceremony.

Several weddings (of friends and acquaintances) have occurred, such as my granddaughter had planned, and while the bride's family could afford the wedding it placed a ridiculous burden on the bridesmaids, all of the wedding attendants, and their families. Many of them could not easily afford the 300 mile trip and three to four day stay at the exotic wedding site.

WEDDING INVITATIONS

Wedding invitations that involve a close family friend and then some multi named bride or multi named groom that we have no idea which name to use in trying to give them a personal gift. Example: you know the groom and his family, whose name is John Smith. He is marrying Jane Marie Marsha White, who you don't know and you are supposed to guess what to call this multi- named bride in a personal gift card or when you see them for the first time. Very thoughtless. (Should highlight "Jane", or "Marie" or Marsha").

OSTENTATION AND AFFLUENCE

For the wealthy to spend on material items and a lavish lifestyle should not be grounds for irritation or peeves. However, the spending in and among those who cannot afford comparable lavish items or lifestyles can be a real irritant and peeve for this author. Schools are the quite obvious place where spending by children can very easily affect all those in a school.

When a great number of students can pay $200 for tennis shoes, $200 for blue jeans and equally high priced dresses, pants and clothes, it is not healthy for those who cannot afford this type of clothing. Of course, the only way to eliminate this sort of difference in the lifestyle of students would be to have school uniforms which is quite prevalent in many other countries and which would be a good thing for this country.

However, we are a long way from getting parents and school boards to arrive at this thinking. More disturbing in schools however, is the huge spending and affluence used at special events. Namely, school proms, graduation parties, and after graduation celebrations by particularly affluent students.

For a student in a senior class to spend $1,000 or soon a prom outfit along with flowers and accessories is bad enough. However, it is much worse and quite prevalent for prom parties to be promoted in such a way as to demand that all those attending spend beyond the ability of a large proportion of the class. In the long run it is more unhealthy for the child who has worn the $1,000 outfit than it hurts the child who cannot afford it. Actually, it hurts the child's parents who cannot afford the expensive prom or party outfit bought by the more wealthy teenager.

A note to this particular irritant and pet peeve is about a principal of a high school in Uniondale, New York who decided opulence was just not correct for his high school.

Kenneth Hoagland, the principal of Kellenberg Memorial High School in Uniondale, New York, decided that the excesses in the Senior Prom which promoted extravagant parties and unsupervised outings for a number of the students costing huge sums of money were beyond that of the average student, although his Uniondale, New York community was quite well to do.

When many parents were personally responsible for groups of their sons and daughters making motel reservations and reservations for three day alcohol related parties and post prom bashes which were dangerous for the health of the children, which he maintained would induce drug, sex and alcohol abuse, he determined that the prom would be cancelled entirely for the following year.

What a great principal with courage.

SPEECH

YOU KNOW

We are not sure when or why the irritating phenomenon of using "you know" occurred. It certainly was not used 50 years ago and prior to and during World War II.

To see some supposedly educated person use the phrase almost constantly is nauseating.

A good illustration that I recall was a teacher at the high school here in Cedartown, Georgia who was frequently interviewed by the local radio station. Every point made, or statement of significance, was followed by "you know".

The temptation is great many times to say 'well I do not know', or 'I did not know'

Teachers and parents should reverse the trend in students and in their personal use.

YOU ALL (MISUNDERSTOOD)

Most in the South are irritated with the misconceptions of the word youall or y'all.

We don't like the use of you all or y'all to refer to a single person, it is plural.

Frequently a person from outside the South will refer to a person, to whom they are speaking, in a derisive manner as "you all" (totally incorrect).

We have a poem which will very clearly explain to those outside the South just how to use the word youall or y'all.

The poem is:

> "Come all of you from other parts, both city folks and rural
> And listen while I tell you this, the word youall is plural.
> When we say youall must come down, or we all shall be lonely,
> We mean a dozen folks perhaps and not one person only.
> If I should say to Hiram Brown for instance, youall's lazy,
> Or would youall lend me your knife, he'd think that I was crazy.
> Now if you'd be more sociable and with us often mingle,
> You'd find that on the native tongue youall is never single.
> Don't think I mean to criticize or act as if I knew all,
> But when we speak of one alone, we all say you, like youall.

If those from outside the South will think only a moment you will realize that y'all or youall is much more melodic than "youse guys" or "youse folks".

"YES" TELEPHONE

How many times have you had someone answer the telephone with just "yes"? Yes what? What are you supposed to answer to "yes"? (A pet peeve).

GUYS

When did "guys" start applying to both sexes? Puzzling when someone says to 2 or 3 women, "see you guys later" or "good luck to you guys".

Whatever became of the distinction – guys and dolls?

JUST PLAIN GOOFY

BATH FIXTURES

The proliferation of impractical, odd, bathroom and plumbing fixtures is inexplicable. The myriad attempts to change from a hot and cold handle in showers, tubs and lavatories to types of "one handle" are very impractical and frustrating. They are much more difficult to adjust and are more likely to be defective and get out of order. If you can't improve on a nice hot and cold handle, don't change to something less practical and more expensive.

How many times have you tried to adjust a one handle shower or tub or a metal combination stopper for the tub?

THERMOSTATS

Quite a peeve is people who don't try to understand thermostats. Too often someone thinks that putting a thermostat above the desired temperature will help it rise quicker. Example: to raise a temperature to 72° it does not get there any faster by setting at 82 than setting it to 72°.

One illustration of a nice lady restaurant owner irritated about her thermostat, was where this author ate breakfast often. One morning there appeared over this usually pleasant woman's thermostat, this note: "Don't touch this damn thermostat." Think she was irritated about tampering with her thermostat?

WATCH CRAZE

Watches of every design imaginable from $100 to $5,000, 10,000, 500,000 and over $1,000,000.

This display of opulence might not qualify as an irritant or peeve except the only purpose of having a $200,000 watch or above, is to show it to someone less fortunate, with an announcement of its costs.

OPULENCE

Does it irritate or peeve you that there is a luxury hotel for dogs and cats? Chateau Poochie in Florida is just that, where the costs of boarding and grooming a pet is as much as for a human at an expensive hotel.

LIGHT BULBS

There are thousands of supposedly funny "how many does it take to screw in a light bulb" sayings. 9 out of 10 are usually devoid of the slightest humor. That doesn't prevent the constant flow of this irritant.

BASEBALL CAPS

They are certainly great for wearing to ballgames, picnics, fishing, golfing, sporting events of all kinds and traveling.

However, I never thought I would see that they would be formal wear in a restaurant during an entire meal. Whatever happened to the tradition of a man removing his cap or hat inside a restaurant or any other building, even in a gymnasium sporting event.

Of course that is trivial compared to the asinine practice of wearing a baseball cap backward. The only way the cap can make the owner look more like a baboon is to wear the cap on sideways.

Seems they are all competing for the "village idiot".

WASTED TALENTS

What an irritant and appalling that a huge unbelievable talent can be wasted by stupid people.

Illustrations, of unbelievable talent being wasted, are Bobby Fischer and Mario Lanza.

Bobby Fischer was probably the best chess player ever, or he could have been. He beat the reigning world champion and then became a psychotic recluse not agreeing to any proper chess matches which would have established him as maybe the best chess player of all time and he has wondered about the world never making use of his great talent and knowledge; totally wasting his life after the championship win.

Mario Lanza could have been one of the best, if not the best, of all singers ever. He was considered to be the equal of the great Italian singer Caruso, considered one of the greatest of all time.

Mario Lanza had the voice to be considered one of the greatest ever and he became a drinking and eating glutton and literally ate and drank himself into a huge weight, literally ate and drank himself to death. What a waste.

The number of great athletes who have wasted their lives from drinking, drug abuse and plain anti-social behavior is too numerous to list.

The reader will notice them every day.

TATTOOS

The use of tattoos is rampant among boys, girls, men and women of all ages, seemingly.

How ridiculous to paint a God given body with awful, indelible, unremovable pictures and designs over one's body.

Some desire to have one's body with freakish designs over it that are different from anyone else is beyond belief and certainly it is not worth having just to endear oneself to anyone looking at it other than some other freak.

BED MAKING IN HOTELS AND MOTELS

Bed make in Hotels and Motels. Do you ever remember getting ready for bed in a hotel or motel that the sheets are not so tightly tucked they must be pulled out the entire length of the mattress before one can get to bed?

Apparently hotels and motels do not study sanitation very much. I am irritated every time I have to take a spread off the pillows. That spread, has been used over and over and is not very sanitary over the otherwise clean pillow cases. Much more thoughtless and more unsanitary is the practice of wrapping the pillows entirely in the spread. Very unsanitary.

Reusable glasses and cups in a hotel are notoriously and inherently unsanitary. Not only are they basically unsanitary, but the horror stories of maids merely wiping them with a dirty rag, are all too frequent.

THOUGHTLESS WEATHER COMMENTS

"What a gorgeous day". Everyone has heard this on a sunny day, when we have been in a drought condition for about 2 years, crops and pastures drying up, lakes and ponds half full, springs and streams flowing at half their previous flow. (Worse from a weather reporter). Thoughtless. The response should be "no, it is not a gorgeous day until it rains".

All weather makes the desert---(Dionysius)

ILLEGIBLE SIGNATURES

Shocked and irritated is a way I describe seeing the signature of many educated people, particularly lawyers, who practiced before my court and with whom I dealt for many years. These lawyers always have a fairly good education and how they can allow themselves to fail to write their name in a legible fashion is beyond my power of reasoning.

If a document is of any value to be signed, the signature should be legible and most bar or court rules now require the signature to be followed by a type written name to identify the signor.

Quite remarkable also has been the history of poor signatures by the medical profession. Historically doctors have been considered the poorest in signing their signature in any profession and in recent years it has been determined that this poor signature practice has resulted in poorly and inadequately and inaccurately filled prescriptions causing illness and death on many occasions. Why this has not been corrected is a tragedy for the public and certainly for the medical profession.

Here is what I consider the most outrageous signature of an educated person that I have ever seen.

Try to understand that this signature is that of a respected Judge.
Evan Esar said: "You can always tell the character of a man by his signature----and sometimes his name".

GLUTTONS (CONTESTS)

How can anyone enjoy watching a table full of humans in a gorging contest in which they see how many hotdogs they can gulp in a short period of time?

"Nauseating" is mild to what this writer feels in irritation while watching grown humans stuffing hotdogs down their throat for some period of time. It seems that participants stuffing food down their throat until their stomach is stuffed is idiotic; it seems that anyone who would enjoy watching this is marginally intelligent also. It seems proper to wish the gorging contestants and also the people who think this is entertainment to both be sick from the whole affair. ,as I am.

INTERNATIONAL

MALTREATMENT OF WOMEN

Failure of the U.S. government and U.S. journalists, editorialists, particularly women writers and leaders, to constantly and positively criticize other religions who approve and practice female circumcision, female mistreatment, beatings by their husbands and treatments as slaves denies them equality in many things. The most important being denying them equal education.

Hypocritical to constantly criticize China on human rights and ignore African , Arab and any country, for this extreme physical and criminal maltreatment of women.

It is my feeling that with more women leaders in the Middle East (and all nations) we would have far fewer wars.

Concerning this leadership aspect, I would tend to disagree with Kipling's :Female of the Species"

"When the Himalayan Peasant meets the he-bear in his pride,

He shouts to scare the monster , who is often turned aside,

But the she-bear thus accosted rends the peasant tooth and nail,

For the female of the species is more deadly than the male."

(If you will pardon a personal note; when this author was District Attorney many years ago, and was prosecuting a woman for murder, on several occasions, it was useful to quote this verse.)

ADVERTISING

FALSE ADVERTISING (MISLEADING OR LYING)

EITHER WAY IT IS AN IRRITANT

Deceptive advertising is an almost daily irritant in the magazines and newspapers and news media in this country.

Illustration number one:this great "apparent charity" says they will give away free Ballistic rolls of new US Government dollar coins. These coins are in uncirculated condition. These free coin rolls are fifty "one-dollar" coins. The person getting the coins for free must pay what is called a $124.00 <u>vault release fee</u> plus shipping, and shipping is not itemized. $124.00 for coins with a face value of $50.00 and of no more value than that at a price of $124.00 plus shipping just doesn't seem to be free, and is an irritant, and a false advertisement.

Under this heading of false advertising, but not as deceptive as the above coin proposal, is a credit card bill One gets some "valuable" customer awards through loyalty to the credit card issuer. These great awards allow one to select any number of magazines risk free for six months. These being nothing but a gimmick to let these magazines promote with a risk free subscription which will continue at their annual price if one does not terminate the subscription. Merely a great advertising scheme for these 58 magazines which the customer does not need. From this same credit card issuer one receives a notice that he can purchase, what looks like, inexpensive jewelry for $9.95. The bracelet, earrings and broach would certainly be a money maker for the credit card issuer as opposed to a reward to me for being a good customer.

Through another mailing as a "customer thank you" supposedly a great reward, one is given the opportunity to buy 8 small items including a set of 4 space saving bags, a cordless power driver, a digital tire pressure gage, any of these 8 items for only $9.97 and they graciously allow you to pick any number of these that you like. None of which seem to be worth more than half of the $9.97 customer appreciation price.

More irritating than all the bank schemes is, with every credit card bill, receiving blank checks pleading with one to borrow money on a credit card, fixed percentage rate, subject to being raised after being caught in the lending scheme promoted by the checks. Undoubtedly, such practices as this are what have created the astronomical debt on credit cards and debt of consumers which has harmed this country.

Mail in Rebates. These are the consumer's "top of the line" irritants. While they are very well legal, they are meant to cheat you out of the price of the rebate. The history of rebates shows that a small percentage of rebates are ever paid. Clark Howard, our consumer specialist in Atlanta, Georgia, of course, despises rebates and gives the logical advice to never buy any article based on a rebate unless you are willing to pay the price without the rebate. Many schemes are used to prevent the consumer from collecting the rebates. Among them are the difficulty in complying with the rules, always confusing, for obtaining the rebate. They are confusing for a reason.

OVERPRICED MAIL ORDER

Overpriced mail order gift items are a real irritant. A box of fruit involving five pairs, two large apples and a dozen or so various cookies and chocolates. All of which could be obtained in a grocery store for about $5.00 and the price to order is $39.95 plus shipping and handling. Then next is a basket of fruit, cheese, smoked salmon and a small amount of cookies and a small box of six chocolates. This basket collection is $79.95 and could be obtained at your normal supermarket for no more than $15.00. This same catalog has some fifteen similar assortments with the assortments being priced about ten times what the collection could be obtained for at a regular supermarket. One supposes we should be more irritated with someone who is too lazy or too thoughtless to buy this at a grocery store, or even at a high priced specialty grocery store, where they could obtain it for a fifth of what the mail order cost is, make a personal package of it, and not have to also pay the exorbitant shipping and handling costs of these expensive treats.

FREE GIFT (OXYMORON OF ALL OXYMORONS)

What person has not received mail that announces they are receiving a free gift. Enclosed will be some name labels or similar item which is not supposed to be a free gift but is only to induce you to send money to them.

Of course, free gift is a poor choice of words. Any gift is supposed to be free and to insult our intelligence claiming that it is free is misleading and an irritant.

Always remember: What the large print giveth, the small print taketh away (Plato).

A few words for all these deceiving schemers: "A half-truth is a whole lie." (Plato, or maybe it was Socrates).

SILLY ADVERTISING

Advertising that will produce results for the company or business is certainly their choice.

It should also be our choice not to respond to any advertising that insults our intelligence and the most irritating of recent advertising is the use of an eight, nine or ten year old to discuss stock and business performance and to allow a ten year old to give her father advice of how to run his business; this advice being the equivalent of what a college graduate would be giving.

Noteworthy is the fact that a company using this silly advertising has had its stock decline drastically.

PRESCRIPTION DRUG ADS

It is an irritant to listen to a prescription drug advertisement and then hear a list of things to "tell your doctor", i.e.: If you have heart trouble, what drugs you are taking, if you have blurred vision, fainting spells, do you have respiratory problems, do you have blood pressure problems. All things a person capable of looking at the television ad and with "half-sense" would tell a doctor without this irritating prompting.

IN STORES

THOUGHTLESS SALESPERSON

Far too common in retail or other stores is the irritant of a salesperson answering, and staying on the phone, while the customer they are supposed to be waiting on stands helpless and his or her time wasted. The customer in the store should have absolute priority over a telephone caller. What are businesses thinking to let this happen?

GROCERY SHOPPERS CAN BE AN IRRITANT

Example: the person at the checkout counter who not only has thirty items or so in the ten item lane but who waits until everything is checked and then decides to look for their checkbook or money or credit card as if it just dawned upon them that they would have to pay.

The people with the broadest beam of all the shoppers also seem to stop with their cart in the exact middle of the grocery store aisle making it impossible to pass and the two town gossips usually find the busiest intersection of the store to prevent customers from passing while they carry on the conversations they have missed for the past week, while preventing shoppers from passing.

BY MAIL

BLANK CHECK IN STATEMENT

Who likes to receive a blank check in every credit card monthly statement, asking the customer to borrow money? This usually at a low initial interest rate, for sure to increase later. This constant pressure for customers to borrow more easy money contributes to the huge credit card debt in the U.S.A.

SURVEYS (MONEY RAISERS)

Is everyone also tired of receiving a "survey" with elaborate stupid questions, requiring an obvious answer: "Do you want your taxes raised to pay someone who has been fired because they were lazy"?

Ending the irritant of the surveys is the plea to send money to this campaign or charity.

MAGAZINES

Most irritating are magazine solicitations for one to renew a magazine subscription immediately and it is still seven or eight months until the subscription expires. A nice little gimmick that is used in this solicitation is that the expiration on the magazine subscription is never shown, encouraging the subscriber to renew many months in advance.

SYMPATHY NOTES

A very personal irritant is to make a donation in memory of a deceased friend whose family one knew very well, sometimes lifetime friends and to receive a form printed note which says "the family of John Smith acknowledges with deep appreciation your kind expression of sympathy". No signature of the family that you know personally. Obviously this is sent from the funeral home or someone just writing them out with no real personal gratitude for the flowers or donation in memory of the deceased.   Very crude and impersonal.

R.S.V.P.

(RESPONDEZ S'IL VOUS PLAIT)

R.S.V.P. What a frequent irritant.

R.S.V.P. is to be used on a personal level when the sender has a relation to the person receiving the mail to respond or in effect be impolite.

For businesses and corporations and charities and any other entities to send a letter with an R.S.V.P. on it, when you have no relation business or otherwise with that organization or that person, is a true irritating insult. An R.S.V.P. should be used for personal or business relationships which are close and which should require a response by the person receiving the mail or notice.

When you receive an R.S.V.P. from any business or person to which you have no obligation to reply; You should not even consider the charity or the organization worthy of reading the letter or notice or document and it should be deposited in the trash because of this irritating abuse of a very good procedure named R.S.V.P.

Wedding invitations, invitations to dinners, invitations to functions where the planner needs to know how many will attend or how many will come to the wedding, the reception, the charitable gathering, the concert or function and they are entitled to know and receive information on those who are coming or will attend is for use of the R.S.V.P. and R.S.V.P. should not be abused for commercial or other reasons.

NATIONAL DISGRACE

ROUNDABOUTS

This is also a deadly and costly irritant in the United States.

The failure to use roundabouts or modern traffic circles at intersections is a national disgrace.
These forms of intersections are used around the world and are only sparingly used in the United States.

It is estimated that we could save some 1,500 highway deaths annually had we developed circular intersections about the country many years ago. We could save some 100,000 major traffic injuries annually. We could save some 60,000,000,000 gallons of gasoline caused by traffic congestion and failing to have circular intersections. We could save some $450,000,000 in electric light energy annually.

We could eliminate tons of pollutants (nitrous oxide) per day and assist all metro areas in meeting federal clean air act standards.

We could reduce the delay and cost per person from traffic congestion now estimated at 36 hours and $625 dollars per person as a national average. We could beautify over 200,000 highway intersections by getting away from the trend to a canopy of traffic lights burning 24 hours a day.

We could save billions of dollars in future construction costs at new and reconstructed intersections.

Why do we not have constant construction of roundabouts or circular traffic intersections? There is no logical excuse for this. Among the feeble, almost childish, reasons are that the engineers do not devote their time to learning about roundabouts, their efficiency and life saving qualities in a child-like reluctance to change from the present system of signalizing every intersection and creating more traffic congestion.

(This author has prepared an extensive manual on this awful irritant).

LEGAL

CAPITAL PUNISHMENT

This chapter (this book) is not designed to argue the pros and cons nor to extensively argue the constitutionality of capital punishment but to point to some legal and mindless irritants.

This author however, believes that capital punishment is not prohibited in any constitution unless it says so. Had the framers of our Constitution desired to classify capital punishment as cruel and unusual they would have said so.

Particularly with capital punishment having been exercised throughout the world at that time and as the prevalent methods of execution at the time seemed to be by hanging, guillotine, and the firing squad; it is significant that none of these were excluded by our Constitution. Absent that, it is evident that the Constitution does not prohibit capital punishment.

There is much asinine trivia in the carrying out of capital punishment.

This does not mean that the author condones awful and horrid torture in carrying out capital punishment but it is a great irritant to see the courts apparently struggle with the nonsensical idea that the injection of a doctor in carrying out a capital punishment order can be cruel and unusual. The argument that the needle is horrifying to the unfortunate defendant is rather absurd. The latest absurdity in court rulings presents this: that the protocol of executing the defendant by lethal injection is cruel and unusual punishment as it "presents a substantial risk of unnecessary pain and violated the death row inmate's constitutional protection under the Eight Amendment." The ruling stated that the new protocol did not ensure that the inmate was properly anesthetized before the lethal injection is administered, which could "result in a terrifying, excruciating death".

To the average citizen untrained in the law this is stupidity. To the average legally trained lawyer or Judge, this is stupidity.

Just a thought in this case, the defendant was convicted and sentenced to be executed because he had beaten an elderly woman to death during a burglary.

No irritant in the law exceeds our current system of endless appeals and habeas corpus reviews which delay finalizing a case for some 10, 15 or 20 years.

The main reason capital punishment is not more of a deterrent is because we have not been able to carry out capital punishment in a decent time frame. The courts have allowed capital punishment opponents to prolong death penalty cases with trivial legal maneuvers such as this lethal injection claim.

SPEEDING LAWS

We should all be irritated to see how impractical and counterproductive we enforce the speeding laws. Most states and jurisdictions of every kind, city, county and federal law enforcements have developed a habit of allowing some five to ten miles over and above the speed limit.

Now this was necessary and reasonable many years ago before the technology was developed to where we can precisely determine the speed of a vehicle. Law enforcement now has the technology everywhere at this time in which to precisely determine the speed of a vehicle on the highways.

What is the effect of allowing five to ten miles above the speed limit before the operator of the vehicle is stopped or arrested?

The significance of allowing anything above the actual speed limit should be an irritant to all of us because it does several things:

(1) It promotes the idea that we can break the law 'some' and not be penalized.

Far above this, and the most damaging of this one type of law enforcement is that we are telling our youth who obtain their driver's license at age 16 (or whatever the individual state determines) that they 'can violate the law some' before they will be stopped.

This psychology is extremely bad for children.

DRIVING WHILE DRINKING

The same horrible psychology that most states use in driving under the influence laws is the same as the speeding psychology. We encourage the drinking public to be cautious in how much they can drink and still drive and stay below the illegal state alcohol level, usually .08% or some beginning at .05%.

I have observed that, "Driving Under the Influence schools" have taught this type of conduct and the defendants have appeared in court and explained how they have been to DUI school and learned just how much they could safely drink and still drive within the legal limits. The legal limit to drive should be that you do not drive while drinking and enforce this as close to no alcohol as practical; maybe not perfect but far above the present psychological invitation to drink "some" and then drive.

COURTS

Among irritants in the court and justice system:

Sentences by a court which are impossible to carry out; i.e.: two consecutive life sentences for murder or life plus 25 years.

This ridiculous practice came from all-powerful Parole Boards controlling the length of all sentences by myriad regulations for releasing prisoners after only a portion of sentences had been served. Court sentences should mean what they say. Prisoners should be released early through court order or earned good time.

DRIVER-INTERSECTION HESITATION

How thoughtless for a driver with a green light, turning left, to fail to proceed into the intersection, but remain at the stop line until oncoming traffic with a green light comes through the intersection.

This can cause vehicles behind to miss one or even two light changes.

Hello Stupid-- pull into the intersection and turn left and help one or two make the light.

JUST PREPOSTEROUS

BEYOND IRRITATING

Some irritants are beyond peeves and are really unthinkable because they are deliberate, directed against another person and intended to harm them mentally and emotional.

The best illustration of this is the late night television host David Letterman. Letterman, in a monologue on his show, stated that the daughter of Sarah Palin (Governor of Alaska at the time) had been "knocked up" by a 'named' New York professional athlete. Supposed to be humorous we presume, but had no humor, no meaning, except vile, despicable invective. This was preplanned and vicious. No apology, no remorse (some late mumbled reason).

Letterman: you are "top of the line irritant", you are scum!

RUNNINGER SECTION

INTRODUCTION

"The measure of a man is the size of the thing that it takes to 'get his goat'," is a slogan I once read. If this is true, I find myself becoming a smaller and smaller person, because as I get old and crotchety, more and more things seem to annoy me, but oddly often amuse me at the same time. I can relate to my late friend Bill Maynard's comment:

"There are three differences in retirement," he once told me. "Two of them are bad, but the other one makes up for it. The first is that you no longer have an expense account to charge things to. That's bad. Secondly, you no longer have a secretary to do all your work for you. That's bad, too.

"But the third one makes up for it! You no longer have to be nice to a single sumbitch if you don't want to!"

People accept the fact that it 's one of the privileges of age to be able to achieve the five "C's" of old age, cantankerous, curmudgeonly, cranky, crusty, and crotchety. Having achieved this age status, I find that the folks I most admire are people like Winston Churchill, who due to his age, was able to get away with "telling it like it is." Examples:

"Clement Attlee is a humble man," he once said. "And with good reason."

"If I was your wife, I'd give you poison," Lady Astor told him." His answer was, "If you were my wife, I'd gladly take it."

Among my other heroes:

"I didn't attend the funeral, but I sent a nice letter saying I approved of it"—Mark Twain.

"He has no enemies, but is intensely disliked by his friends."—Oscar Wilde.

"He is a self-made man, and worships his creator."—John Bright

"I've just learned about his illness. Let's hope it's nothing trivial."-- Irvin S. Cobb.

"He has delusions of adequacy,"—Walter Kerr

"Thank you for sending me a copy of your book. I'll waste no time reading it."—Moses Hadas

Come to think of it, it may be best to delete that one, since I hope that lots of people will waste their time reading this book.

Anyway, that's what the following section is about—the joys of getting old enough to be able to get pissed off about lots of little things.

FOLKS WHO TALK TOO MUCH

They seem to forget that the Lord gave them two ears and only one mouth for a reason. When I was in optometric practice, with some folks typically taking a case history went like this:

"Do you have any health problems, Mrs. Gabble," I would ask.

"Well, let's see," she replies. "I did have a little cold, that started a week ago Wednesday. No, it couldn't have been Wednesday, because that's the day I get my hair done, and I remember I felt fine that day. So it must have been Thursday. Or maybe Tuesday……………….ad infinitum.

I'm afraid I'm also guilty of this at times:

"Exactly what is astigmatism?" a friend once asked me. So I gave him a five minute technical explanation.

"I'm kind of sorry I asked now," he said when I had finished. "I really didn't want to know that much about it!"

FOLKS WHO TALK TOO LITTLE

In contrast to Mrs. Gabble, I once asked a male patient about his health, and he replied, "It's fine." When his wife came in the exam room, she asked:

"Did my husband tell you about the concussion he got last week, and his very high blood pressure, and his recent heart attack, and his diabetic condition?"

The ultimate in giving incomplete information----Rural folks here in the NW Georgia mountains have a tendency to be rather taciturn. Two of them met in town one Saturday.

"Hey Jed," said one. "What was it you give your mule when he had distemper?"

"Turpentine," was Jed's answer. A couple of months later they again ran into each other on another Saturday visit to town.

"Hey Jed. I give my mule turpentine like you said, and it killed him."

"Killed mine too," said Jed.

GLOOMY PEOPLE

I have enough of my own problems. I don't need to commiserate with folks who always complain, and see the dark side of things. A few minutes in their company, and I get the blues too.

Try this test. Look around the room for 15 seconds looking for anything that has the color red in it. At the end of the 15 seconds, I ask you how many things you also saw with the color blue in them. You probably don't know, because red is what you were looking for.

In the same way, in life's situations you find what you look for. If you look for doom and gloom, that's what you're going to find. If instead you look for the bright side, that's what you'll find instead. You'll be a happier person and also one who people like to be around.

"We'd be a lot happier if we concentrated on our blessings as much as we do our problems," I once heard a preacher wisely say.

"They told me to cheer up, things could be worse," reported one optimist who had learned to laugh at his problems. "So I cheered up, and sure enough, things got worse."

PESSIMISTS

I hate being around folks who always assume that things are always going to turn out bad. Like the traveling salesman who had a flat tire while driving home about dusk one evening. When he looked in the trunk of his car, he discovered that he had left his jack at home.

The road was little traveled, and no other motorists came by to give him help. Then he noticed the lights of a farm house about a mile or two across a field. The only solution he could see was to walk across the field to the farm house, borrow a jack, and return to his car to change the tire.

But by the time he had walked part ways across the field, the lights in the farm house went out.

"Oh, oh," he said to himself. "Evidently they've all gone to bed and by the time I get there, they'll be asleep. I'll have to pound on the door to wake them up, and that's going to make them mad. Then when I ask the farmer if I can borrow his jack, he's going to cuss me out for waking him. We'll get in a big argument, and maybe even come to blows.

The more he thought as he walked, the madder he got about what he envisioned was going to happen. When he finally got to the house, he pounded angrily on the door. He heard an upstairs window being raised, and a voice said, "What can I do for you?"

"I just wanted to tell you," the salesman heatedly responded, "where you can stick your damned jack!"

Much better is to be an optimist like the surgeon who had been in partnership with a pessimist for many years. They were summoned to the emergency room one evening.

"Your friend Phil Landerer is in bad shape," said the emergency room physician. "He was visiting a Susie Sexton on 14th Street, when her husband came home unexpectedly and found them in bed together. He emptied his revolver into Mr. Landerer, and since he is a friend of you both, I thought you'd like to check him.

"Well, things could be worse," said the optimistic partner after their examination.

"I'm sick and tired of your always saying things could be worse!" exploded the pessimistic partner. "You know our friend is going to suffer horribly and then die. And that he has no insurance to support his wife and three small children. And that they are going to have to live with the shame of all the publicity this will receive. Just how could things be worse?"

"Because if it had happened last night rather than tonight, it would have been me."

TOILET SEATS

One of the most universal pet peeves from the female gender seems to be males who leave the toilet seat up. Why is that our responsibility? Why can't we males complain about women who leave the toilet seat down?

"You can't satisfy wives," said comedian Rodney Dangerfield. "My wife always complained about me leaving the toilet seat up. So I have since remembered to put it down. Now she complains about having to sit on a wet toilet seat!"

PEOPLE WHO DON'T USE DEODORANT

On an extremely hot day in Atlanta one summer, a "ripe" country boy got on a packed elevator. His aroma was not exactly that of Chanel #5.

"Someone forgot to use their deodorant," declared a miffed lady on the elevator.

"Tweren't me," said the country boy. "I don't use the stuff myself."

BRAGGARTS

Some folks delight in one-upmanship. Whatever they have or do, is much better or smarter than you.

A friend told me of such a man he knew in Atlanta who had a Volkswagon, and kept boasting of his gas mileage. (Which reminds me of the Chrysler Imperial I used to have that got 20 miles to the gallon. Eight in town and twelve on the road.) His neighbor got tired of hearing him brag, and decided he'd give him something to really boast about. Early every morning, he'd sneak into the neighbor's garage and add a half gallon of gas to the car's tank.

Now the neighbor was bragging about getting 70 miles to the gallon! After two weeks of this, the neighbor began siphoning out a half gallon of gas every morning. The owner drove himself and his mechanic crazy trying to figure out why he suddenly was getting only twelve miles to the gallon.

Some folks like to brag about what great wheeler-dealers they are. I've discovered a system that can deflect this.

"I bought this oriental rug for just $1200," they tell you. "Guess how much it's worth now?"

They of course want you to make a low estimate, like maybe $1800. Then they can triumphantly say, "Nope. It has quadrupled in value!"

Instead you purposely way overestimate, and say innocently, "Gee, I don't know. $100,000?" This takes the wind out of their sails, and they will no longer bother you with tales of their business acumen.

Another example: "My new car lists for $32,000. Guess how much I got it for after dickering with the dealer?"

"Gee, I don't know," you say again innocently. "$12,000?"

"This card says I am a leader of men and irrestible to women!" bragged a man as he stepped down from a scale that gave weight and fortune.

"It has your weight wrong too," said his wife as she read the card.

Even braggart's wives get tired of the boasting.

PROLONGING BORING SPEAKERS WITH INANE QUESTIONS

The speaker has been a nightmare. Not only was he boring, but he talked about 20 minutes over his limit. He finally finishes, as you breathe a sigh of relief, and finally can leave. But instead:.

"Does anyone have any questions?" he asks before sitting down. "No, no, no!" I say to myself. But I'm wrong. Some idiot decides this is a good time to show off his knowledge on the subject, so he proceeds to ask a lengthy question, which is really more a statement than a question. The speaker, pleased to find that he has "reached" one of the audience, then responds with another ten minute talk, while you entertain thoughts of annihilating the questioner before he can ask another stupid question, and prolong the evening even further.

The same principle applies with untalented entertainers. I was attending an elder hostel session a few years ago. The entertainment one evening was a lady soprano who had difficulty in finding the right key. After she had off-keyed for almost an hour, she asked if anyone had any requests. One joker kept asking her to sing additional songs, which she did with relish. My friend, Dr. Bill Baldwin, finally figured how to end the misery. When the singer asked if anyone else had a request, my friend spoke up:

"Yes. I'd like for you to sing Good Night Ladies!"

BORING, LONG WINDED SPEAKERS

Two optometrists were on a plane on the way to attending an educational congress, when the plane was hijacked by some terrorists.

"To show we mean business, we're going to kill two passengers," said one of the terrorists. The two they selected were the two optometrists. "But just to show that we're not completely hard hearted, we'll give each of you a final request."

"Before I die, I'd like to have the satisfaction of making the two hour lecture on glaucoma I've worked hard to prepare for the meeting we were going to," said the first OD.

"Permission granted," said the terrorists. Turning to the second one, he asked, "And what is your last wish?"

"I've heard this guy's lectures before. My request is that you kill me first so I don't have to listen to him again."

Many times I've felt almost the same way. Too many speakers and preachers reach a perfect stopping point, or even say "In conclusion", and then keep talking for another 10–15 minutes.

Funerals are one of the worst culprits. When I go, I have left instructions that the memorial service be no longer than 25 minutes. I've had to sit through too many hour and a half services, which always seemed to me would be embarrassing to the departee. In one of those, there were three preachers with long messages, plus an old friend who regaled us for 30 minutes with boring stories of things he and the departed had done together. I was sitting with my crusty friend, the late Judge Jimmy Dick Maddox. At the 90 minute mark when one of the preachers launched into another sermon, Jimmy Dick gave a sigh of exasperation, and got up and walked out.

Which reminded me of what Robert Benchley once did when he was a theater critic. He was reviewing a particularly bad play. In the second act. A native girl said, "Me Melona. Me good girl. Me stay."

"Me Bobby. Me bad boy. Me go," Benchely announced loudly as he got up and left the theater.

"That was a terrible speech," said a man to the long winded speaker at the end of the meeting.

"Don't pay any attention to him," the program chairman said. "He's half witted and doesn't know what he's saying. All he ever does is repeat what he hears everyone else say."

PEOPLE WHO WON'T ADMIT THEY'RE WRONG

"That's the Young mansion coming up on the left," said the bus driver, as he drove the tour group through a neighborhood of movie stars' homes many years ago.

"Robert Young?" asked a lady.

"Nope. Loretta Young. And on the right is the Barrymore estate."

"Ethel Barrymore?" inquired the same lady.

"Nope. John Barrymore. And on the left, you'll see the famous Christ Church."

"Try again, lady," said a voice from the back of the bus. "You can't be wrong every time."

I may be stupid at times, but I don't enjoy admitting it. So when I'm wrong like this lady, I am sorely tempted to make excuses or refuse to admit it. But as my granddaughter, Jody Watson, points out, this alienates other folks, and is one of her pet peeves.

Dr. Richard Carlson in his book "Don't Sweat The Small Stuff says, "One of the most important questions you can ask yourself is, 'Do I want to be right---or do I want to be happy.' Many times, the two are mutually exclusive. Needing to be right ---or needing someone else to be wrong---encourages others to become defensive."

Recently I was playing tennis against my friends Bubba Dunson, and Dr. Bob Williams. We disagreed on the score, and argued vociferously about it. Suddenly I realized that they were correct and I was wrong. So remembering what Dr. Carlson had said, instead of refusing to admit it, I told them, "Much as I hate to admit being stupider than two guys like you, I have to admit that you were right and I was wrong." Dr. Carlson was right. It felt good to admit the mistake. And it caused them to no longer be angry with me.

"Only mistake I ever made was the time I thought I had made a mistake, but really hadn't," said one always right culprit.

RUDE PARKERS

My wife, What's Her Name, (I can't use her real name, because she tells me she'll pound knots on my head if I write about her) likes everybody, and I never knew could ever be peeved by anything. But she tells me her pet peeve is when she waits patiently for the car that is leaving a parking space in a crowded parking lot, so that she can take over the space. Then as the car leaves the space, before she can pull in, a car coming from the opposite direction whips in ahead of her.

This reminds me of the jerk who was late for a very important appointment, and couldn't find a parking space anywhere near the building in which he was supposed to meet. After driving around, in desperation he looked skyward and said, "God, if you'll just open a parking space for me, I promise I'll give $10,000 to the church. And I also promise to attend church every Sunday."

Lo and behold, a space immediately opened up right in front of the building. "Never mind Lord," he said. "I've found a space.

Another parker who is a peeve, is the one who, in a crowded parking lot, parks straddling the line, thereby taking up two spaces. And people who leave grocery carts in a parking space, so that there is no room for a car to park.

And of course, able bodied people who park in a handicap space so that they won't have to walk too far. Have you also noticed how many people will drive around the parking lot for 15 minutes, seeking a close parking spot in order to keep from having to make a two minute walk?

IDIOT DRIVERS

A driver peeve of mine is the tailgater. I'm always tempted to stop quickly so he'll smash in the front of his car before he can brake. Fortunately I remember that this will also smash in the rear of my car, so would probably not be a wise thing to do.

Dr. Len Werner says his peeve is the driver who continues sitting at the red light when it turns green because he is busy talking on his cell phone. Conversely there is the guy behind you who leans on his horn if you don't move the nano-second the light changes.

The late Nick Powers once pulled up at an intersection, and noticed that the car ahead of him at the stop light was being driven by his friend Dot Hogg. So being a smartass, he kept honking his horn at her as soon as the light changed. The lady looked around to see what idiot was honking incessantly. Nick was horrified to note that she was not Dot Hogg, but instead a lady he had never seen. He tried to shrink down in his seat as she continued to stare at him rather than proceed through the intersection.

You are driving down the road. You come to a sign that says, "Right Lane Closed Ahead, Merge Left." So everyone slows down and merges into the one lane. Except for the idiot who whizzes past you in the right lane, figuring that someone will let him squeeze in at the head of the line. I tend to drive in such situations with half the car in the left lane so I'm still in line, and the other half in the right lane to try to block such drivers. Usually doesn't work. They'll go off the pavement to get past me.

It's bad enough when drivers talk on their cell phone while driving, taking one arm away from the steering wheel, and making them concentrate on their conversation. I read somewhere that cell phone talking drivers cause as many accidents as drunk drivers.

Now, even worse, (As pointed out to me by Dr. Stan Yamane) we have drivers who are texting while driving, taking their eyes off the road periodically as well.

Perhaps my main driving irritant is drivers who think that when the traffic light turns from green to yellow while they're half a block away, it 's a signal for them to speed up to get through the light before it has become red for too long.

And drivers who pull into an intersection, thereby blocking traffic when the light changes.

I did, however, hear of one bad driver I kind of admired. He was eating a steak at a truck stop, when three motorcycle hoods came into the restaurant and began to pester him. One emptied an ashtray into his coffee, another stole his steak, and the third poured catsup on him. But he never reacted or defended himself and instead left the restaurant.

"He sure wasn't much of a man not to defend himself against us," said one of the motorcyclists to the counter man.

"He isn't much of a truck driver either," he replied. "He just ran over three motorcycles as he left the parking lot."

PEOPLE WHO CAN REMEMBER NAMES

"Why did you kick that turtle?" asked one elephant of another.

"Because he bit me on the toe back when I was just a baby, 30 years ago."

"How can you possibly tell it's the same turtle?"

"Because I have 'turtle' recall."

As I get older I find I no longer have 'turtle' recall, or even partial recall when it comes to people's names. That's why I hate folks who do remember names. They make me look bad. I'm always afraid not remembering names might lead to even worse problems. Like:

"First I started not being able to remember names. Then faces, and then to zip up," once said the late Sam Levenson. "Now it's gotten worse! Yesterday I forgot to unzip."

"I think it is so tender that you still call your wife 'Honey' and 'Darling' after over 50 years of marriage," a sweet young thing said to an old timer.

"I have to," he replied. "I can't remember her name."

There are many name recall systems out there. I've tried most and find they have one thing in common---they don't work. For example I heard about the Jim Farley system, and figured it would be foolproof. (Jim Farley was a master politician back in the days of Franklin Roosevelt). He reportedly could remember thousands of names. But when he couldn't recall the name of someone he had previously met briefly, he would say, "I'm afraid I've forgotten your name."

"I'm Cedric Hoople," the person would say, for example.

"Why Cedric, you didn't have to tell me your first name," Farley would reply. "It was your last name than had slipped my mind."

The very next day, I ran into a distinguished elderly lady patient, who I had known for many years. I needed to introduce her to my wife, but had no idea what her name was. So I figured I'd use the Farley System, and said, "Gee, I am so sorry but I'm afraid I've forgotten your name."

"Mrs. Turner," she replied in a hurt tone.

I was halfway through my Farley response, before it dawned on me that, "Why sure, I remembered the Mrs., it was your last name I couldn't recall,' was not going to be exactly an erudite response.

I discovered a few years ago at my DePauw University 50th college reunion that when someone is inebriated, it makes the problem worse. "If it isn't old Henry Harris," an obviously soused classmate greeted me. "You sure have changed. You used to be shorter and fatter and had a bigger nose."

"I'm not Henry Harris, I'm Jack Runninger," I told him.

"Changed your name too, huh?" he replied.

Another system I tried was the Association Method, in which you associate something about the person's appearance with his or her name. I never could remember the name of a local citizen, named John Massey. Finally I noted that he was tall, like Abraham Lincoln. And I remembered that in movies years ago, Lincoln's part was often played by actor Raymond Massey. Using this association, I henceforth remembered his name.

I admitted to the aforementioned John Massey at a party one night of how I had used this system to recall his name. "I wondered why you'd been calling me 'Raymond'," was his response.

Another danger of this is the Freudian slip. Years ago there was a wonderful local citizen, Johnny Beane. He was an alcoholic, but had been able to overcome it and did marvelous rehabilitative work with other alcoholics for many years.

The emcee at a United Fund luncheon introduced him to the audience as "Jim Beam." (For my non-drinking friends, Jim Beam is a brand of whiskey.)

An elderly friend told me he had started taking memory pills to see if it would help him remember names. "Has it worked?" I asked him.

"I don't know," was his reply. "I never can remember to take them."

A man I recently met told me he had a foolproof system for remembering names, and that if I'd remind him, he'd send it to me. I wish I could remember his name.

MR. GUNDERSON

When I was in high school, my physics teacher was Mr. Gunderson. He used to continually tell us, "Enjoy yourself while you can. Your high school years will be your happiest time of life. You'll never be as happy again after you become an adult. (I think he was a high school football star, and nobody paid him and his lousy personality any attention after that.)

"Geez, I have enough problems now," I'd say to myself, as I'd leave his class, extremely depressed. "If things are going to get even worse, there doesn't seem to be many rays of hope in the future."

Fortunately, shortly thereafter I came under the influence of Reverend Joe Claire, who conducted a class for teenagers every Sunday night at his church. Joe Claire was an Englishman in his sixties, had a jolly face and rosy cheeks, and had an enormous head topped by a wild thatch of snow white hair.

He always wore a derby hat, and it took a size 7&7/8 to fit him. Anyone who might have put it on by mistake would have found it down over his ears and eyes. Yet such was his impish humor, he had an unexpected (for a preacher) card inside the hat that read, "Like hell it's yours, put it back."

"Don't let anyone tell you that your teen years will be happier than your adult years," he told us one night. "You have so much to look forward to: Selecting your life partner, the joy of children and grandchildren, the sense of usefulness and independence you don't have now, increasing wisdom, and so many more things."

He made me feel so much better, and I've found he was right. I've found that every age has its advantages and disadvantages. For example, I don't think I could stand going back to my teen years, and having to begin the dating process all over again.

When I was about 14, I discovered that a girl named Helen Judt all of a sudden became more interesting than footballs and baseballs. And a helluva lot prettier! I sat at the phone every night for three weeks trying to get up the nerve to call her for a date. I finally made it, but remember sounding like a gibbering idiot on the phone. I also recall being a little bit less "couth" than Mortimer Snerd on the date. The shock of the whole experience was so great, it took me six months to again ask anyone for a date.

There are advantages to every age, so enjoy the one you're in, and look forward with hope to the future. And ignore folks like Mr. Gunderson.

MY WIFE'S FIRST HUSBAND

"No matter how hard we try, it is impossible to be perfect," said the preacher during his sermon. "Is there anyone in this congregation who feels that he or she is perfect?" One gentleman stood up.

"You claim to be perfect?" asked the preacher incredulously.

"No," he replied. "I'm standing to represent my wife's first husband."

This story insinuates that the man's wife is always telling him how much better was her first husband. That's not the case with me. But I knew my wife's first husband for many years before he passed away, and there has never been a more good natured, pleasant, and popular person, without a single enemy. It irks me having to try to live up to that, instead of being my normal cantankerous self. There has only been one other person I've ever known who didn't have an enemy.

"No matter what you do," thundered another preacher, "you cannot please everyone. Is there anyone in this congregation who can honestly say he does not have a single enemy?" One old gentleman in the back pew stood up.

"Do you maintain," said the preacher incredulously, "that you don't have even one enemy?"

"Nope," replied the oldster. "I outlived ever' one of the s.o.b.'s"

Despite having this difficult first husband to live up to, my second marriage has been a most happy one. Not at all like the gentleman who was hugging a gravestone in the cemetery. While crying hysterically, he kept saying over and over, "Why did you have to die, oh why did you have to die?"

"Your wife's grave?" asked a lady bystander sympathetically.

"No," he sobbed. "Her first husband's."

PEOPLE WHO RESENT PREACHER JOKES

A preacher had a conflict with the Board of Deacons, and they fired him. His last Sunday he preached on the importance of righteous living:

"Just because you're a church member doesn't mean you won't go to hell if you don't live right," he explained. "And even though I'm a preacher, if I don't live right I could go to hell.

"And the Board of Deacons can go to hell, too!!"

Why is it that preachers seem to be the butt of jokes more than any other profession? Does it mean there is a lack of respect for the ministry as some long faced folks seem to think? I don't think so. Religion should be a happy and positive thing rather than gloom and doom. The "Thou shalts" of religion are a lot more important than the "Thou shalt nots". And kidding and jokes are a part of a happy and positive relationship.

Like the story of the young preacher whose first assignment was to a small country church. He was extremely nervous about his first sermon, so decided he should open with a thunderous Bible quote to get off to a good start.

"BEHOLD I COME" he shouted as he began the sermon. Then his mind went blank, and he couldn't remember what came next. So he started over.

"BEHOLD I COME" he again proclaimed. Again his mind went blank. So again:

"BEHOLD I COME," as he frantically leaned too hard on the pulpit. With that, the pulpit gave way and he went tumbling into the congregation, ending up in the lap of a little old country lady in the front pew. As he apologized to her, she said:

"Tweren't your fault, Preacher," she replied. "I shoulda got out of the way. After all you told me three times you was a comin'."

Many of the preacher stories center on deflating the pompous ones. Such as: "I have sad news for you," intoned such a pompous one at the end of a sermon one morning, "The Lord Jesus has called me to another church, and this will be my last Sunday with you."

"Let's all stand," said the choir director as the preacher sat down, " and sing 'What A Friend We Have In Jesus.'"

To their credit, almost every preacher I've known has taken the kidding good naturedly. And some are right good at giving it back. A number of years ago, the late Wright

Bagby, Sr. introduced the Rev. Forrest Lanier as the Lions Club speaker one noon. Wright was a master at "giving the needle", and his introduction was a masterpiece of disparaging remarks and preacher jokes about Forrest, (who was his pastor and good friend).

"Now I know how the Philistines felt," said Forrest as he began his talk, "when they were smitten by the jawbone of an ass."

TV EVANGELISTS

And their eternal sobbing requests for money. They remind me of a device I once saw that was labeled as the world's most useless instrument. All it did was when you flipped the switch to the "on" position, a hand came out of the box, turned the switch back to the "off" position, and then retreated back into the box.

I am reminded of this device whenever I see some TV evangelists spend most of their air time pleading for contributions in order to pay for more air time to plead for more contributions to pay for more air time, ad infinitum.

"Time is growing short, and the devil is winning because you have not sent us a pledge," I once saw Jim and Tammy Bakker plead with tears in their eyes. "We need your financial help in order to destroy the devil so we can complete our building project," lamented Jim with quivering chin.

Evidently they must have rallied in the bottom half of the ninth to defeat the devil. I saw in the paper a few months later that not only had they raised sufficient funds to complete the project, but had enough left over to buy themselves an expensive condo in Florida.

Ernest Angley was exceptionally effective, with his healing services. All you had to do was place your hand on the top of your TV while he cried "HEAL", and you were automatically cured of whatever problem you had.

"Can you pray for my hearing?" a shady looking character reportedly asked him on one of his shows. Angley smote him on both ears while yelling "HEAL". Then he asked him, "How is your hearing now?"

"I don't know," he replied. "It doesn't take place until next Wednesday at the courthouse."

DIFFICULT CAB DRIVERS

"Why is the airport so far from town?" a friend told me he asked his cab driver on the way from O'Hare Airport to downtown Chicago.

"I don't know," the cabbie responded. "I guess it's because they wanted to put it where the planes land." It reminded me of some of my experiences over the years. Chicago's cabbies seem to be the worst. The last time I took a cab from the airport there, the driver I had was a sinister looking guy with long, greasy, stringy hair.

It was a harrowing experience! Not only did he dart in and out of traffic at 85 MPH. In addition every time he passed a car, he would turn his head and leer at its driver. Perhaps it's just superstition, but I tend to get nervous when a 3,000 pound vehicle, in which I'm a passenger, goes hurtling at super sonic speeds, through heavy traffic, while its driver is leering to the rear, rather than pointing his eyes in the direction he's going.

The other Chicago cabbie I remember was a lady (using a very loose interpretation of the term "lady"). I served in the US Navy during World War II, and figured I'd heard all the experts in the use of salty language. But this gal could hold her own with any of them! In addition, she had the disposition of a rattlesnake with a belly ache.

To make matters still worse, this was in December, the temperature was minus five degrees, and she kept opening her window to hurl her string of vituperation at anyone who got in her way. She was even ready to stop and fight another cab driver, until I convinced her that he was probably a golfer, and what he had hollered at her was "Fore!", rather than "Whore."

Another friend said it was in Chicago that he asked his driver to stop and clean off his filthy windshield so he could see where he was going. "Wouldn't do any good," the cabbie replied. "I forgot my glasses anyway."

And some will take advantage. A tourist reportedly hailed a cab at the train station, and gave the driver the name of the hotel where he would be staying. The hotel was right across the street, and the cab driver readily perceived the man wasn't aware of it. So he drove him around town for a long time, before delivering him to the hotel, and told him the fare would be $38.

"You must think I'm some sort of rube that you can take advantage of," hotly proclaimed the passenger. "Last year when I was here, the cab fare to the same hotel was only $29."

Every once in awhile you'll get a comedian, who makes fun of such practices. When I was in Cork, Ireland a few years ago, we hailed a cab to return to our hotel. "Do you know how to get to your hotel?" he asked us. We told him we did.

"That's a shame," he replied in a pleasant Irish brogue. "I was plannin' on takin' you the long way, so I could charge you more money."

GULLIBLE FOLKS

"Why is your left ear bandaged?"

"I was pressing a pair of pants when the phone rang. I got confused and held the hot iron rather than the phone to my ear.

"What happened to your right ear? It's bandaged, too."

"He called back."

Most folks are not this stupid, but all of us do stupid things at times.

For example, most of us tend to be too gullible.

Reportedly a student at Eagle Rock Junior High won first prize at the Greater Idaho Falls Science Fair. In his project he urged people to sign a petition demanding strict control or elimination of the chemical "dihydrogen monoxide." His reasons:

1. It is a major component in acid rain.
2. Accidental inhalation can kill you.
3. It contributes to erosion.
4. It can cause severe burns in its gaseous state.
5. It has been found in tumors of terminal cancer patients.

He asked 50 people if they supported a ban of this chemical. 43 said yes.

Six were undecided. Only one realized that "dihydrogen monoxide" is a chemical term for water. The title of his project was, "How Gullible Are We?"

This is a good example of how messages can be slanted, or even sometimes plain lies. Honest people have a tendency to trust other folks, and thus believe anything that's in writing or that they're told. Unfortunately the world doesn't work like that any more.

In a newspaper column in the Rome (GA) News-Tribune I once kiddingly told the old joke about a man who stole a can of peaches. I said that Judge Walter Matthews had sentenced him to four days in jail, one for each of the four peaches in the can. And that his angry wife had then said, "Your Honor, he also stole a can of peas."

A few days later, a lady who obviously doesn't understand that you can't always take literally things said by idiots like me, asked the judge, "Did that really happen?"

Another example happened years ago in the Los Angeles Times newspaper. In the classified ads ran an ad that said, "Last day to send your dollar to Box 173." Hundreds of people sent a dollar to the perpetrator of the idea.

THOSE WHO FEED ON THE GULLIBLE

The whole gullibility problem has become worse with the advent of the internet and e-mail, with its inundation of sappy and usually untrue sentimental claptrap, political exaggerations, etc. (This is the reason for one of the most important rules of life, "Never give your e-mail address to a retired person!)"

For example, during the 2008 campaigns I kept receiving e-mails maintaining that Hillary Clinton was the only senator refusing to meet with representatives of the Gold Star Mothers because of her hate for the military. Now I am far from being a devotee of Mrs. Clinton, but fair is fair, and the story happens to be a complete falsehood according to www.snopes.com.

And then there are the saccharine phony inspirational stories. I received a new one the other day, with the author's assurance that it was true, and the usual admonition that I must send this on to a least 10 others, to prove that I am a caring person. As I recall, it also harped on what a cad I was if I didn't do so. But at least it didn't assure me of receiving a miracle by 4:00 PM if I forwarded to the 10.

A lady was mountain climbing when her contact lens came out, and fell hundreds of feet below. "Lord," she prayed, "You know every stone and leaf, and you know where my contact lens is. Please help me."

When she returned to the base camp that evening, she found that an ant carrying the contact lens on its back had brought the lens back to camp. (Must have been "Super Ant").

Another story that has circulated on the internet so often that it has been accepted even by intelligent people as being true.

The story, in one of its versions, goes that when Winston Churchill was just a boy, he was saved from drowning by a poor farmer. So thankful was Winston's father, Randolph, that he insisted on paying all future education costs for the farmer's son.

The boy was Alexander Fleming, who because of this education went on to discover penicillin. Further, that later in life, Winston Churchill contracted pneumonia and that his life was saved by massive doses of penicillin. A touching story. Only problem is that it's not true.

Paul Harvey told the story on the radio, and I heard a preacher deliver it from the pulpit. But again, it is not true.

There is one of these syrup email stories that I did enjoy. It pictured a cute little teddy bear saying, "Click on my tummy for a sweet message." When I did so, the cute bear turned into a snarling ferocious bear, saying, "Get your #$%&@#$ hands off my belly, you #$%&@#$ pervert!"

LOOKING FOOLISH

The blacksmith picked up a horseshoe to inspect it. By mistake he got a red hot shoe just out of the forge. He of course dropped it immediately with an oath.

"Pretty hot, wasn't it?" laughed a bystander.

"Naw," replied the smithy. "It just don't take me long to inspect a shoe."

I guess I'm not alone in trying to cover up dumb mistakes by pretending that's what I intended all along. "I had gone into a store to run an errand," a lady told me. "I came back to the car, opened the door, slid in, deposited my package on the right hand seat, and reached for the steering wheel and to insert the key in the ignition.

"Only there wasn't any steering wheel or ignition there! I had climbed into the back seat, rather than the driver's seat."

She took the coward's way out, yea, even as you and I would have done. Rather than embarrassedly and immediately moving to the front seat, she first busily began searching through the packages in the back seat. Thus any passer by would assume that she had purposely entered the back seat to look for a particular package.

I know just how she felt. I once had a similar experience in Scotland. I am not a complete idiot, and do know that the driver's seat is on the right side in British cars, since they drive on the left hand side of the road. This fact had brought forcefully to my attention my first day in London, when I was horrified to see a Great Dane sitting on his haunches and driving a passing car! Until it dawned on me that the left front seat he was occupying was not the driver's seat as it is in the U.S.

Anyway, habit is a powerful thing, so I automatically piled into the left front seat of the rented car I was picking up. "Mygawd, they've given me a car without a steering wheel," I panicked momentarily before realizing what I'd done.

Did I immediately slide over to the other seat, thereby admitting my lack of savoir faire? You can bet your sweet bippy I didn't. Instead I began to busily search the glove compartment so that bystanders would not realize I was a hick tourist who had goofed.

Another way of getting out of embarrassing situations is to shift the blame elsewhere. I am not the most proficient member of a local performing singing group. Thus I am inclined to make an occasional error. Such as coming in a measure early, while everyone else is of course silent. When the audience looks in my direction, I've found it effective to turn a horrified and accusing stare on either Dr. Joel Todino or Eric McDowell, the two singers on either side of me.

I always enjoyed the Andy Griffith show episode in which they were forming a church choir. There was one voice that was horribly out of key. So Barney Fife told Andy that in place of singing, he would wander behind the choir to find out who it was. He never could figure out why the off key voice disappeared when he quit singing and tried to find it.

DOUBLE LAST NAMES

Recently there was an article in the paper about a lady who felt it was unfair for her newborn child to have only her husbands' last name. Evidently the father agreed, or got tired of arguing about it, so they gave the child the last name from both parents.

I think the lady is correct about the injustice of children carrying only the father's last name. But if her idea catches on, we're in BIG trouble. Let's say that Adam McDougald marries Eva McCorkle. They name their son McKensey McDougald-McCorkle Later McKensey marries Esther Davidson-Dunson. Their child becomes Mabel McDougald-McCorkle-Davidson-Dunson.

In just a few generations you could have a kid with a name something like Dan Hanks-Clark-Green-Shapard-Stewart-Fowler-Rogers-Sumner-Bosworth-Self-Newman-Mahaney-

Minge-Dempsey-Allen-Bagby-Reynolds-Slickman-Gates-Davidson-Todino-McDowell-Wright-Edwards-Watson-Nordeman-Adams-Melton-Rutledge-Fambro-Sweitzer-Baldwin-Hancock-Ballou-Odil-Kendall-Noth-Hortman-Redwine. (I use these friends' names in hope that it might bring them fame and inspire them to purchase a book.)

Perhaps a better solution would be to combine both parents' names for the offspring's first name. For example, Ferdinand and Eliza Smith could name their child Ferdiliza.

There seems to be a lot of interest in tracing family names. It always seemed to me that a similar problem applies here. By the time you go back five generations, the guy with your family name is responsible for only 1/32 of your bloodline.

"A rose by any other name would smell as sweet," is an oft quoted Shakesperian phrase. The implication is of course that the label has nothing to do with the qualities of the thing or person. I don't know that I agree. It appears to me that people may often live to their names.

Doesn't it seem likely that the same person would behave differently if his name was Reginald VanSnootingham than if it was Hiram Snagglewart?

Fortunately, if you have a name you don't like or is too cumbersome, you can go to court and have it changed. I've heard a rumor that this is what one local citizen did.

"I hate my name and want to change it," he told Judge Bob Walther.

"What is your name," he asked.

"Burgett Wojeickowinweskobramovitch."

"I don't blame you for wanting it changed. What new name have you chosen?"

"Joseph Wojeickowinweskobramovitch."

PHONING THE DOCTOR

Back when I was in optometric practice, if a patient wanted to ask a question or advice, he or she would phone the office and leave word with the receptionist. Then as soon as I had time between patients, I would return the call. Sounds easy enough. But modern life with all its conveniences has screwed up the whole thing.

Last week we tried to reach What's Her Name's doctor with an important question. So I phoned his office. What I got was an automated message asking me to press the key for the department I was seeking. Naturally, this was the last one, number 9, which I then pressed.

I was anticipating talking to a human presence. But, you guessed it, I got another automated message asking me to press the key for the source I wanted. "Talk to the doctor" was not one of the options, so I figured the closest thing to it was to request the "Talk to the nurse" option.

But evidently the nurse didn't want to talk to me. After 20 minutes of listening every minute to another automated voice say, "Your call is important to us. Please hold and we will be with you momentarily." But they weren't. I found myself so frustrated by the whole process that I began talking to the recording like it was a human being.

"If my call is so damned important to you," I found myself yelling at it, "why in hell aren't you answering it?!"

SMARTASSES

This may be more of a jealousy than a peeve. I hate it when people "one up" me with clever smartass answers. Some examples follow:

When I became engaged to be married a couple of years ago, I discovered that I really do have a smartass group of friends. Some of their comments:

"Where did you find a blind woman?"—Charlie Davidson

"You'd better get hitched in a hurry before she comes to her senses."—Bobby Kane.

"I'm thrilled for you but not for her."—Gardner Wright

"She could have done much better than you."—Dr. Floyd Roebuck. Which seemed rather unkind coming from a man of the cloth.

"Obviously she is a former optometric patient of yours, and thus can't see what you look like."—Pierre Noth

"Please give her my condolences." Ed Edmondson.

"Congratulations," said Ruth Martin to me. Then turning to my future bride, she said vehemently, "Have you lost your mind?!"

But I guess I'll have to admit to being a bit of a smartass myself, because in answer to the above barbs, I told everyone that my fiancé and I had first met at a party recently. And that she had immediately said to me, "You look exactly like my second husband."

"Indeed?" I replied. "How many times have you been married?"

"Just once," she said. Before I get scalped at home, I hasten to state that this is not true.

"You sure did clear up my dry eye problem," a patient once told me.

"I'm glad the eyedrops helped so much," I replied.

"It wasn't the drops that did it. What happened was that when I got your bill, it was so high it brought tears to my eyes."

Another office incident: "My eyes tear up with these contact lenses when I play golf, and I have to take them out," the late Billy Camp told me.

"That's ridiculous," I told him. "Professional golfer Dr. Gil Morgan wears contacts when he plays, and he's a top money winner."

"Yeah, but you didn't fit his."

Kind of like the story about the man who told his surgeon that he was still having pain two weeks after the surgery.

"That's nonsense," said the surgeon. "I had exactly the same surgery last year, and had no pain at all."

"It wasn't exactly the same. You had a different surgeon than I did."

"Have you lived here all your life?" I once asked a new acquaintance.

"Not yet" was his smartass reply.

An English optometrist told me of a new patient who had to spell his name for them. "It's W-R-E-S-T-O-N," he said. "But the W is silent---like the P in swimming."

One of my favorites---"I've been waiting for you all day," the state patrolman said with relish to the teenager he had stopped for speeding.

"Well, I got here as quick as I could," said the boy.

- Atlanta Constitution columnist, the late Leo Aikman once told of the lady at the zoo who couldn't understand why the monkeys were not in the front of their cages where she could see them. So she asked the zookeeper why.

"It's mating season," he told her, "so they're back inside."

"Do you think they would come out if I threw them some peanuts?" she asked.

"Gee, I don't know, Lady. Would you?"

- The San Diego Wild Animal Park a few years ago was looking for a good name for their monorail. They emailed their employees asking for suggestions. One employee's reply read "WGASA." Zoo officials loved the African sound of the name, and thus named the monorail "WGASA" as the man suggested.

Only problem was that the employee had not meant it as a name suggestion. Instead, what he was conveying was the initials for "Who Gives A Shit Anyway."

STUPIDITY

I probably shouldn't get upset with stupid folks, because they probably can't help it. Yet there are times their statements/actions can't help but irritate. A few examples:

- "A lady phoned my office to make an appointment," a New Jersey optometrist told me. "My receptionist asked her if she had been to our office before.

"She answered in the affirmative, so we searched patient records in the computer, but couldn't find her. After a failed exhaustive search of the files, we asked her if she was sure she had her eyes examined here.

"'I never had my eyes examined here, but I was here with my cousin when she had her eyes checked a few years ago.'"

- Another occurrence was told to me by a local dentist. He told of a man coming to him with the complaint that his false teeth were uncomfortable.

"When I looked in his mouth, I discovered what had to be the worst fitting plate I had ever seen. So I asked him what jackleg dentist had made them.

"You did!' he said emphatically.

"I couldn't believe I had ever done such a lousy job of fitting, so I asked him when I had made the teeth for him."

"You didn't make them for me, you made them for my wife. She died a few weeks ago, and I figured I'd use them since she don't need them no more.'"

- The lack of knowledge of medical terms is often amusing rather than irritating. Various optometrists have reported examples to me:
- "I take a 'precious' (blood pressure) pill every morning."
- "As a child I had 'romantic' (rheumatic) fever."
- "My son was very ill a few years ago. He had 'Spirit Mighty Jesus.' Turned out she meant "spinal meningitis.
- "A little old lady told me that her vision had been poor ever since she had had a 'detached rectum' (detached retina)," Optician Jolly Wansley told me.

Many times the dumb answers/actions come from children because of their lack of experience, rather than stupidity.

- "One day in our pediatric clinic," reported a medical technician, "I handed a young lad a urine sample container, and told him to fill it up in the bathroom. A few minutes later he returned to my nurse's station with an empty cup."

"I didn't need this after all," he explained. "There was a toilet in there."

- "How old are you?" I once asked a boy I was examining.

"Five," he replied.

"When will you be six?" I asked in order to put his birth date on his records.

"On my next birthday," he replied with a "That sure is a stupid question" expression on his face.

PEOPLE WHO THINK I'M STUPID

As I get older my sense of hearing just isn't what it used to be. Thus I often find myself in groups not fully comprehending what's being discussed, because I don't hear all of the conversation. It irks me when other folks interpret this miscomprehension as being due to senililty rather than hearing loss.

- A example of how making sense from a conversation can be a problem with hearing loss: Author Will Stanton tells of meeting at a party a British lady who had purchased a neighboring farm with a very old house on it.

"Are you enjoying your new home?" he asked the lady.

"Very much," she said. "We have ghosts, you know."

"No," he replied, "I didn't. It's funny I've never heard about them before."

"They weren't there before. We brought them with us."

"We had one in the house when I was a boy," said Stanton, in an attempt to humor the lady's obvious belief in ghosts. "Sometimes I could hear it in the attic. Sometimes it would even come into my room."

"And it didn't bother you?"

"Oh, no," said Stanton. "I've always been quite fond of them."

Just then the lady's husband came up. After introducing him, she said to her husband, "Mr. Stanton and I have been having the most extraordinary conversation about goats."

There are other problems involved with hearing loss:

- One is the misunderstanding of questions asked. We used to tell the story on the late John Read about him telling me of the marvelous new hearing aid he had purchased. "It cost a lot, but it's well worth it," he reported. "My hearing is completely restored."

"That's great," I told him. "What kind is it?"

"It's a quarter to three," he replied, glancing at his watch.

- Medical Economics once told of the elderly woman who was undergoing a physical exam. "Big breaths," said the physician as he placed his stethoscope on her chest.

"Yes," she sighed. "But you should have seen them 40 years ago!"

- This always reminds me of another elderly lady's health exam. It may not exactly qualify as a hearing problem, but I feel impelled to tell it anyway.

"How long have you been bed ridden?" the MD asked her.

"Not since my husband died 10 years ago," was her reply.

- Even more of a problem is the misunderstanding of medical instructions. Dr. Frank Stegall was walking down the street one day when he encountered an 88 year old patient of his, prancing down the street with a young peroxide blonde on his arm. "What do you think you're doing?" he demanded of the elderly gentleman.

"Just following your instructions," he replied. "You told me to be cheerful and get a hot momma."

"No, no, no!" responded Frank. "What I told you was, 'Be careful, you've got a heart murmur.'"

- Another problem is the difficulty of keeping up with hearing aids since they are so small and easily misplaced. And expensive! George Home once told me of a gentleman undergoing an ear exam.

"Why do you have a suppository in your ear?" asked Dr. Stu Smith.

"Thank God," replied the gentleman. "Now I know where I lost my hearing aid."

- Comedian Jackie Mason reports another concern.

"There were a lot of kids in my family. The reason was that my mother was hard of hearing. Every night when they went to bed, my father would say, 'Do you want to go to sleep, or what.' Since she couldn't hear him, she'd say, 'What.'"

- Reportedly some people don't mind losing their hearing. "Mr. Jones, you're going to have to quit drinking," Dr. Toby Morgan told a patient, "or you're going to lose your hearing."

"That's okay, Doc, "replied Mr. Jones. "What I've been drinking is a whole lot better than what I've been hearing."

I'll close this section with a valuable word of advice. When I or any other hard of hearing person sits next to you at a play, a movie, a board meeting, etc., run, don't walk to a different seat. It will save you from an evening of responding repeatedly to their saying "Woddidhesay?"

PEOPLE WHO THINK REDNECKS ARE STUPID

A number of years ago the late Nick Powers and I were asked to write an illustrated joke book for the ultimate redneck, TV star Junior Samples. Junior and his manager came to Nick's farm for us to discuss the project. When I arrived, Junior in his bib "overhauls" was wading around the edge of Nick's fishing lake, pulling "turkles" out of nests dug into the bank. While helping pull him out of the lake, I fell and cut my hand on a sharp rock.

"We've got some 'store bought' whiskey in the trunk we can pour on the cut to disinfect it," said Junior's manager.

"Hit works better," said Junior, "if you swallow hit and let it work hit's way out to the cut from the inside."

"Do you want one of the 'turkles' (large turtles)," he asked me.

"How do you eat them?" I asked.

"Hit takes purty sharp teeth," he said as he tapped the shell.

Most city folk view rednecks as ignorant hicks, and tend to ridicule them. To the contrary, I think Junior's clever replies illustrate that while rednecks have less book larnin', many are sharp people. Even though they are rural, outdoor people, with limited educational opportunity and thus not grammatically perfect, they have more intelligence and abilities about the basics of life than do city dwellers.

What I like about them is they are not pretentious, "put on" folks. What you see is what you get. Another great attribute is their sense of humor and lack of worrying about political correctness. They have the ability to laugh at themselves, a la exaggerated Jeff Foxworthy stories. Such as:

"If your Halloween pumpkin has more teeth than your wife, then you may be a redneck."

"If your toilet paper has numbers on it, you may be a redneck."

"If you think the last line of the Star Spangled Banner is 'Gentlemen, start your engines', you may be a redneck."

"If you keep staring at the orange juice can, because it says 'concentrate', you may be a redneck."

Most other ethnic groups seem to have lost this important facility to not take themselves too seriously.

My redneck friend Bud Sims illustrates the self-deprecating redneck sense of humor: He tells of a couple of friends who were lamenting the fact that their wives seemed to be the boss in their households."

"Bygawd it ain't that way at my house," interjected Bud. "I run things at my house—the vacuum cleaner, the washing machine, the lawn mower….."

In addition to rednecks, many people take delight in ridiculing the supposed stupidity of some celebrities. They love to make fun of baseballer Yogi Berra for example who supposedly once said, "Nobody goes to that restaurant any more, because it's too crowded."

I met Yogi when he was a coach for Houston and they came to Atlanta for a series with the Braves. My friend Kerry Yencer was the sports editor for the Rome News-Tribune at the time, and took me with him when he went in the locker room to interview Yogi.

"You recently made the smartest comment I've ever heard," I told him. He looked surprised at someone labeling him as smart for a change, and asked what it was.

"It was when you said, 'I didn't say all those things I said.'" To me it was a great way of humorously stating that he had not said most of the sayings attributed to him. The guy is dumb like a fox, and his sly grin confirmed it.

Lots of "stupid" folks are a whole lot smarter than the people who accuse them of being stupid.

VERBIAGE SHOWOFFS

I recently received a form letter written by our U. S. of A. government. After wading through approximately 1,000 words of legalese, I finally figured out that all it said was, "Send back the enclosed form with your social security number if you don't want taxes withheld on your savings account interest."

I sometimes feel that nowadays we are drowning in a sea of words. Among others, government agencies, lawyers, and yea, we in the health care professions seem bent on snowing folks under with a surplus of complicated verbiage. The purpose of language is to communicate ideas to other people. Thus it does seem logical that we should state things in the simplest manner possible for the best chance of being understood.

The late Dr. A.M. Skeffington was a brilliant researcher in developmental vision and psychological optics. His problem was that he never used a one syllable word if he could find one with five syllables to use. A number of years ago I was toastmaster at the banquet for a meeting at which he spoke. I read up on his writings, and wove many of his favorite big words into a story I told on him at the banquet. I think it illustrates that simple language is a whole lot better method of getting your point across.

I maintained that I once wrote Dr. Skeffington for advice. I outlined my exam findings on a case, and asked him if he agreed with the lens Rx I proposed.

"Your proposed Rx," wrote back Dr. Skeffington, "will alter the photon scatter on retina in such a way that it will change the input-output-feedback sequence. The resultant spatial distortion will cause biochemical and biophysical changes and this stress produced constriction will make the labyrinthine and kinaesthetic circuiting out of balance with gravity."

"Thanks for your advice. I'm glad you agree with my handling of the case," I wrote back, completely misunderstanding what he was saying.

"You have misconstrued my advice," he rushed a second reply. "The Rx will alter the centering-alignment-identification cycle, interfering with the organism's spatial invariance and degrees of freedom to operate within his operational visual space world. This space volume distortion will interfere with his vestibular-antigravity processes."

"Thanks again for your help, and I'm glad you still agree with my lens Rx for Mr. Jones," I replied.

"Let me put it this way," said Skeffington in his third reply, finally getting his point across to me. "If you prescribe the lenses you propose, they will make Mr. Jones dizzy as hell!!"

People also need to judge their audience in communicating with them. A redneck is not going to understand the same vocabulary as would a college professor.

The late Nick Powers and I wrote a book entitled "Favorite Jokes of Mountain Folks in Boogar Hollow." In doing the research it dawned on me that many of the stories had to do with the misunderstanding of big words. Two examples:

- A salesman got aholt uf Cousin Ebb t'other day 'n tole him, "Now thet you got kids in skool, you oughta buy them a encyclopedia."

"Nothin' doin'," sez Cousin Ebb. "Let 'em walk to school like I did."

- Ole Man Barton's gal Susie almost drownded a'swimmin' in the crick las week. Ther wuz a college boy a'swimmin' wid her 'n he reskewed her 'n got her to breathin' agin.

She wuz kinda weak so this here boy carries her in hiz arms up to the Barton place. He sez to Ole Man Barton, "I'se jest resuscitated yo daughter."

"Bygawd," sez Ole Man Barton, "yewer a'gonna marry her then!"

UNSOLICITOUS SOLICITORS

It appears to me that charity isn't near as charitable as it used to be. For example, it appears that national charities have evolved into becoming high-pressure business's, often with more money spent on expenses and salaries that what goes to the charity itself. My peeve is that once you contribute to these charities, you then seem to get on a sucker list, and become a target for constant bombardment by mail and phone to give even more.

For example, I had always given a fairly substantial yearly gift to the American Diabetes Association. The only time they ever expressed appreciation was as a prelude to asking for more. Even though I try to explain that I am giving only a yearly gift, they evidently figure I am a wealthy and forgetful philanthropist, and continually throughout the rest of the year bombard me by mail and phone for further contributions. The mail is bad enough, but it's the endless phone solicitations that really irks me.

A few years ago, I gave what I considered a generous yearly gift to the American Cancer Society. Six weeks later I received two missives from them on the same day. One reminded me that I had not made my yearly contribution—I suspect they figure a certain percentage of donors won't remember, and give again.

The other letter was one thanking me for my yearly contribution. Included was a letter asking me for a further contribution.

Their high pressure hasn't worked on me. I now give nothing to either organization, despite the good things they do, so they'll leave me alone. Which they don't.

I am a firm believer in the good accomplished by the Salvation Army. (As an example of their good work, a friend phoned them and asked, "Do you save bad women?" When the reply was in the affirmative, he continued, "Great. How about saving me a couple for Saturday night?")

But they are also one of the culprits. I give generously to the United Way, which is supposed to finance such local charities. Nevertheless, I also gave a yearly gift to the Salvation Army. This did not preclude a couple of additional fund appeals from them in the next month, and a request for my yearly renewal gift less than two months after I had already given it.

But in defense of these charities' irritating solicitations, they may think them necessary because so many folks are like the gentleman who complained to a friend, "My wife is always asking me for money. It's continually 50 bucks here, and 25 bucks there."

"What does she do with all that money?" asked the friend.

"I don't know, I never have given her any."

CHEAPSKATES

"I'm collecting contributions for the Widow Jones. She is ill, lost her job, has three small children, and is going to be evicted from her apartment tomorrow unless she can come up with her rent payment."

"That's awfully nice of you to be so concerned about her welfare," said the other gentleman. "You must be a very good friend of hers."

"No," he replied. "I'm her landlord."

People seem to be more selfish and less charitable than they used to be. Another irritation I have is folks who give a small amount to any fund drive that comes along, whether they're important or insignificant. They'll give the same 10 bucks to any request, whether it's something vital like United Way which is raising money for many agencies, or an appeal for the Home For Wayward Cats.

Speaking of United Way, when prospective donors were being researched, it was noticed that a very wealthy attorney had never contributed. So a team was sent out to try shame him into giving.

"Do you realize," he said in response, "that my brother has cancer and needs a very expensive operation, and has no insurance to cover it?

"And do you realize that my sister is a widow and dead broke, and has three children who require expensive schooling because of their special needs?

"And do you further realize that my mother has no income and no insurance, is ill, and needs around the clock nursing care?"

"I'm so sorry," sympathized one of the solicitors. "We had no idea of all your financial woes. We apologize for having asked you for a contribution."

"So if I refuse to give any money to any of them," the attorney continued without pausing, "what makes you think I'd give any to you?"

I must admit that I was also once uncharitable a few years ago while attending a meeting in Portland, Oregon. A seedy looking inebriated gentleman approached me on the street, and asked me to give him money for food.

"You'd just spend it on liquor," I refused him.

"I would not!" he declared indignantly. "I already have the money for that!"

DOCTORS WHO MAKE ME WAIT

I realize that emergencies arise, and doctors cannot always stay right on schedule. But too often they seem concerned only with their time and scheduling, and not that of their patients.

A physician's nurse once told me he could see me at 11:00 the next day. So I rearranged my schedule and cancelled appointments I had during that hour, in order to get there on time. And waited, and waited. In discussing with other waiting patients, it became obvious that their office had made 8-10 appointments for the very same time, evidently so they'd have a steady flow of patients in case any showed up late.

I had to wait an hour and a half to be seen, and was not a happy camper. I changed physicians and never went to him again.

I have always enjoyed the true story that happened in Florida a few years back, about an engineer who had an appointment with an ophthalmologist, and had to wait two hours to be seen. He then sued the M.D. for $200, maintaining that he charged $100 an hour for his time. Rather than go to the expense and time to contest the suit, the doctor had to pay him the 200 bucks.

COMPLAINERS

I, as do you, hate to have to listen to people who are always griping about something or other. Although come to think of it, their complaints are at times justified. For example: "My knee still hurts six weeks after the knee surgery you did on me," a patient complained to his surgeon.

"Nonsense," replied the surgeon. "I had exactly the same surgery, and had no pain at all after the first week."

"Yours wasn't **exactly** the same," said the patient. "You had a different surgeon than I did."

Another great illustration of justified complaining is the old story about the novitiate in the monastery whose penance was to spend his first seven years in silence. At the end of the seven years, he was called before the monks, who told him, "You are permitted to say two words before entering another seven year period of silence."

"Bed's hard!" he said.

After the second seven year silence, he was again permitted to say two words.

"Food's bad!" was his answer. And then he was sentenced to another seven years of silence. At the end of this period, he was again given the chance to say two more words. Which were:

"I quit!"

"You might as well," said one of the monks. "You've done nothing but gripe and complain ever since you've been here!"

CONFUSING RELIGION WITH MAGIC

My favorite religious story, with a great moral lesson often forgotten, is about the man who bought a rundown farm in Coweta County. It had been abandoned for ten years, and was in terrible shape. The fields were grown over with weeds, bushes, etc., the house and barns were in terrible disrepair and falling down, and the yard a tangled mess.

For the next two years he labored night and day to restore the farm. The house and barns were rebuilt and painted, the front yard cleared, grassed, and flowered, and the fields cleared and producing crops. The new preacher came to make a call on him after he had completed his work.

"My," said the preacher, "the Lord certainly has blessed you with this beautiful farm!"

"Mebbe so," said the farmer. "But you shoulda seen this place when the Lord had it all by hisself!"

"I notice that when I pray for the Lord to send me a chicken, I never seem to get me a chicken," said the chicken thief. "But if I prays to the Lord to send me after a chicken, I usually gets a chicken," is a similar example.

It seems to me too many people expect the Lord to magically provide without any effort on their part, contrary to the lesson learned by the farmer and the chicken thief.

A close Jewish friend told me of the Orthodox Jew who had no job and spent all of his time studying the Old Testament. He fell in love with a young lady, and asked her father for her hand in marriage.

"How do you plan to support her?" asked the father.

"God will provide," answered the suitor.

"Does your daughter's fiancé like you?" a friend later asked him.

"He really does. In fact he obviously thinks I'm God."

One further story I think also illustrates the fact that the Bible is often considered some sort of magic, rather than a guide to how to live:

"What can I do?" lamented the man to his preacher. "I've gambled away all my money, lost my job, my wife has left me, my house has been foreclosed, and I'm dead broke."

"Perhaps the Bible can help," said the preacher. "I would suggest that you open the Bible at random, and without looking, place your finger on a page, and see if God gives you a message as to what to do."

A few months later the gentleman returned to the church. He was wearing beautiful clothes, had a gorgeous new wife, and was driving an expensive new car.

"I see that my advice has worked," said the preacher. "May I ask what words you pointed to in the Bible that gave you guidance to solve your problem?"

"Where it said 'Chapter 11'."

SELFISH RELIGION AND CHARITY

"Have you done your good deed for today?" the scoutmaster asked the three cub scouts.

"Yes," they replied, "we took a little old lady across the street."

"Why did it take all three of you?"

"Because she didn't want to go."

Too often charity and helping are performed by people just to make them feel good, rather than to help others. A number of years ago Marian Wilder told of a happening that made a great impression on me. She and a companion had taken a meal to a destitute shut in. The lady thanked them, and then said:

"I want to give you this jar of peanut butter". Marian thanked her profusely as she took the jar.

"Why did you take the peanut butter?" asked Marian's companion after they had left. "She needs it far more than you do."

"Because she also needed the satisfaction of doing something for someone else, just as we did."

A great point! Charity givers are often motivated to give to make themselves feel good, rather than what is best for the one receiving. We need to remember that it is natural for those receiving charity to feel somewhat ashamed to be the recipient, rather than having the joy of being a giver.

"God saved my life, and I am so thankful," wrote a news correspondent a couple of years ago. "I was riding in the rear of a truck in Iraq. We stopped to pick up two soldiers, who got in the truck bed next to me.

"We hit a roadside bomb a short time later. The fragments from it hit and killed the two soldiers standing next to me. If it hadn't have been for God protecting me by instructing the driver to stop for the two soldiers, I would not have been shielded by them, and would have un-doubtedly been killed. That's why I'm so thankful to God."

The two deceased soldiers may have possibly had a different view of the goodness of God. Too many folks think God is centered on them more than on other people. Many times you have heard people who were spared in a tornado or other disaster say that it was God who had saved them. Why would He save that person, but let all the others die?

Probably in this "selfish religion" category also lies the lack of tolerance different religions and churches have for each other. They feel theirs is the only way. For example I heard this story from an Irish Catholic when I was in Ireland:

"What have you been doing since you were last home ten years ago," the Irishman asked his daughter.

"I've become a prostitute," she confessed, breaking into tears.

"How could you do this to your family?" he thundered. "You are no longer welcome in this house!"

"I'm so sorry to have been a prostitute," she tearfully apologized.

"Prostitute? Oh, that's okay then. I thought you said 'Protestant'!"

MY TIME IS YOUR TIME?

I hate folks who seem to think their time is worth more than mine, by habitually showing up late. This was also mentioned to me as pet peeves by Dr. Len Werner and Dr. Mel Wolfberg.

Even worse is the following scenario: You are called to the phone by your secretary. "Mr. Bigshot would like to speak with you," she says. So you pick it up only to hear the voice on the other end say, "This is Mr. Bigshots secretary. He'd like to speak with you. Please wait just a moment while I locate him."

This is rude! When he's the one making the call, I expect him to be on the phone when I answer, not make me wait while he is located. I have found a way to handle this. When I hear from the secretary, "Mr. Bigshot would like to talk to you," I answer, "I would certainly enjoy talking to him as well. Please tell him to call me when he has the time." And then hang up.

ORGAN RECITALS

Not the musical kind. Instead, vital organs. Dr. Ben Milder named and reminded me of this one.

"How are you?" you say to an acquaintance you meet on the street. You don't really want to know, it's just a form of greeting. Unfortunately some people respond to this question with a thirty minute description of all their health problems, when you really didn't want to hear a description of their headaches, hemorrhoids, etc. Or in Dr. Milder's play on words, an "organ" recital.

TV REMOTES

Why do I have to use more than one remote control to watch television? Not only its inconvenience, but I also invariably punch the wrong button on one of them at times, which screws up the whole thing, and takes me 30 minutes to find what's wrong. It appears to me that modern science should be able to develop a single, simple control for idiots like me.

A NIGHT OUT

You look forward to a nice peaceful, romantic dinner with your spouse so both of you can relax after a hard week. You pay a lot of money for a baby sitter so you can have this quiet time together.

And where are you seated at the restaurant? Right smack next to a couple with three small loud and misbehaving children. Parental control is completely lacking, because the parents obviously think that the cute little darlings are cute and entertaining to the other restaurant patrons.

DISHONESTY

It was almost closing time at the butcher shop, and the butcher had one chicken left that he wanted to sell before it went bad. Luckily, a lady came in and said she wanted to buy a chicken. So he produced the lone chicken and weighed it at four pounds.

"Do you have one just a little bit larger?" asked the lady.

"Yes ma'am," he replied as he removed the chicken from the scale, hid it back in the case, and then brought out the same lone chicken. As he placed it on the scale, he also exerted slight pressure on the scale, so that it registered five pounds.

"That's fine," said the lady. "I'll take both."

I think it's great that dishonest folks, like the butcher, usually get their comeuppance sooner or later. Another illustration of this happened to my usually honest friend, Dr. Conney Batson, a retired veterinarian when he was still in practice.

It had been a particularly busy afternoon, and they didn't finish with the last appointment until 6:30. The phone rang just after his employees had all left, and he was on his way out the door. He figured it might be his wife, Carolyn, calling to find out when he'd be home, so he answered it, "Batson Animal Clinic."

"Oh, Dr. Batson, I'm so happy you're still there," he heard a female voice say. He recognized the voice. It was a lady who was a nonstop talker, and would keep him on the phone forever, and possibly even ask him to stay while she brought in her poodle.

He mentally processed all this information and came up with a solution in only about one second's time, so he smoothly continued, "This is a recording. Our office is closed. Please call back tomorrow." He settled back in his chair, congratulating himself on coming up with such a quick solution.

"What?" he heard the lady say. Without thinking he replied:

"I said this is a recording, please call back tomorrow."

PHONE NUISANCES

I'm expecting an important call. As always it comes at an inopportune moment, such as when I've gone to the bathroom. I rush to get to the phone before it hangs up, only to discover the call is some recorded message or a marketing call, rather than the call I was expecting. It's kind of childish, but I don't hang up on the marketing calls. I leave the phone off the hook while I go elsewhere, so that the marketer can spend a few minutes talking to thin air before he or she realizes it. I figure that is time they would otherwise be utilizing to bother someone else.

Automatic fax machines that call my home number, particularly late at night can also cause me to fume.

Another phone irritant is when people leave their name and phone number on my answering machine, but talk so fast and/or softly you can't understand them, and have to listen to the message multiple times to try to figure it out.

BUSINESS BUZZ WORDS

When articles contain such buzz words as "synergisitic", "globalize", "paradigm shift", etc., it seems to me the author is concentrating on showing off how smart he is, rather than trying to impart his or her message.

SHOW OFF ATHLETES

I particularly hate while watching golf on TV, the golfer who sinks a putt and then does a vigorous fist pump, so observers will realize how great he is.

And you are probably as irked as I by football players who point to the sky and excessively celebrate after scoring or making a tackle. As one coach said, "It's more impressive if you act like you've been there and done that before." Which reminds me of what famed football coach, the late Blanton Collier, once told me irritated him:

"Pass receivers who 'hear footsteps' as they go across the middle on a pass route. They realize they're going to get clobbered as soon as they touch the ball, so they're thinking about that rather than catching the ball. We used to tell them, 'You're going to get clobbered whether you catch the ball or not, so you might as well concentrate on catching it and getting credit.'"

INSECTS

This one on insects came from What's Her Name. I was relieved to discover I was not one of the insects to which she referred, but instead the flying and crawling types:

"Tiny gnats too quick to swat."

"Walking into spider webs."

"Yellow jackets on your food and drink." A friend had it even worse. He didn't notice a yellow jacket on his can of coke. When he took a sip, the yellow jacket registered its displeasure with having to share, and he was "stung on the tongue". (I like the way these two words rhyme with each other.)

USELESS AND MADDENING WORDS

I once heard a pro football player being interviewed. In the two minute interview, he interspersed 34 "you knows" into his replies. In the same category is the overuse of the word "like", which seems to have infected our teenagers in recent years. "I'm like telling her, you know, to like leave me alone," doesn't make a whole lot of sense to me.

INAPPROPRIATE CURSING

Cussing in public should also be a no-no. It's not that I give a damn, but it sounds like hell to others.

BOASTING ABOUT GETTING DRUNK

I think it's kind of stupid when guys brag about how drunk they got last night. Or back in their college days, etc. It's not that difficult an accomplishment. All you gotta do is drink too much. Plus to me it should be a source of embarrassment rather than acclaim.

HOUSEHOLD PARAPHERNALIA

There have to be gremlins residing in my house. I have a desk on each side of my office, so have a ten foot telephone cord so it can reach both. Each day I take the phone off the hook, and carefully straighten out the coiled cord. The following morning the gremlins have completely knotted it up again. The effective length of the cord has become less than two feet, as I discover when moving the phone to my ear pulls the base off on the floor.

The other household peeve is the drawerful of unknown cords, adapters, and other electrical devices. I don't know what any of them are for, but am afraid to throw them out, because I'm certain if I do, I'll discover I need them later. It appears to me that they mate at night, because the accumulation seems to multiply without my adding anything to it.

A SWEET WIFE

You may find it odd that having a sweet wife would be a pet peeve. And at most times it really is a blessing. But at times she can drive me crazy by being so thoughtful and tender.

This noon we laid down to take a nap. As usual, as soon as we dropped off to sleep, the phone rang. Now when I'm napping alone, I just ignore the ring, and go right back to sleep. But What's Her Name seems to think it socially incorrect not to answer the phone.

"Gee, you'll have to speak with my husband about that," I heard her say sweetly, after listening to the other party for 2-3 minutes. Another pause while she listened, and then she said, "He's taking a nap right now. Can you call back in about 30 minutes?"

Then she listened to the other person for another few minutes, and finally repeated sweetly, "Can you call back in about thirty minutes?" And then durned if she doesn't listen for another three or four minutes, before again apologetically requesting the other party to call back.

"Who was that who called and kept talking to you even after you thrice asked them to call back?" I asked, figuring it must have been an important call. It turned out it was a telemarketer who had already bothered me three times that week.

"Why didn't you just hang up?" I remonstrated.

"Because that would have been rude," she replied.

BARBECUE SIGNS

It seems as though every barbecue joint sign I've ever seen includes the image of a happy pig. What does the pig in a pork barbecue have to be happy about?

RATE INCREASES

When a utility sends you a letter about a rate increase, why does the explanation always open with, "In order to serve you better………." They have never asked me if I would like to pay more for better service, nor told me how the service is going to be better.

WIVES' ANSWERS

"Do I turn left at the next intersection?" I asked my first wife a few years ago, as we drove to some destination that escapes me at the moment.

"Do you mean to tell me that you have lived in Rome, Georgia for almost 50 years and still don't know how to get to where we're going?" said she.

"Look, I was not requesting a discussion of my admittedly poor sense of direction," I unwisely replied. "The only response I was looking for was whether or not to turn at the intersection, which we have now passed, so it's too late to find out anyway."

Somehow we finally got to where we were going, but not via wifely directions since she wasn't speaking to me by that time.

Anyway it got me to thinking---Why do wives always answer a question with a question rather than an answer. If I had asked a male companion the whether or not to turn question, he would have solved the problem with one word, either "straight" or "left". I have a friend with the same problem. He once asked his wife:

"Why do you always answer my questions with another question?"

"Why do you ask?" she replied.

DOGS

"Agent Zloty, after your reconnaissance of the planet Earth, what can you tell us about the dominant species there?" asked the commandant from outer space.

"The dominant species is obviously a four legged furry specimen, known as 'Dog'," he replied. "These dogs are so much in control, that they have trained an otherwise intelligent species know as 'Man', to be completely subservient to them, and to feed, house, and support them without their having to do a lick of work.

"In many cities, they have even trained 'Man' to suffer the humiliation of following them on their walks with an instrument called a 'pooper scooper', to clean up any deposit they make."

I think maybe Agent Zloty is correct---that dogs are smarter than humans, and that we're in danger of being taken over by them. According to a news item I read, some futurists predict the number of human births will slow in the 21st century. So much so that the world's population will level off after the year 2035.

But according to The Futurist magazine, replacing the people population explosion will be a quadrupling of "companion animals" during the century. The problem as I see it, is that if dogs are really as smart as some of their owners make them out to be, with their increasing numbers they may soon take control of the world.

But perhaps it's not that dogs are smarter, but instead that some dog owners are stupider. Often otherwise perfectly sane people become blithering idiots when speaking of, or to, their canine friends.

The comic strip "Marmaduke" invites readers to send in examples of the cute things their dogs do. A random sampling of some of these cute things their dogs have done includes:

- "When company comes, Sophie says 'hello' just after having had a drink, and dribbles in the company's lap and down their legs." (I'm sure the recipients of the dribbles find this adorable.)
- "When I was having lunch with my husband, Duke grabbed a sandwich out of my hand, and ran out the door." (This is cute?!)
- The most important event in Shana's life is her evening walk. Pattie could walk her all afternoon, but if she doesn't get her at-dark walk, she pouts." (Pouts?!)

"God must have loved dogs, because he gave them His name spelled backwards," wrote a lady in a letter to the editor of a publication that had run an article she considered unfair to dogs.

Not only talking "about" their dogs, but the manner in which some owners speak "to" their dogs is idiotic. "All I Really Need To Know I Learned In Kindergarten" author Robert Fulghum wrote, "I'm embarrassed by how people talk to dogs, I really am," said Fulghum.

"Especially when people do this ventriloquist act where they speak to the dog, and then answer for the dog in another voice: 'Does Poochie wantum drinky? No, Poochie wantum go outside.'"

LASSIE TV PROGRAM

"I blame much of the animals-are-smarter-than-humans movement on the old TV show, Lassie," wrote Sarasota Herald-Tribune columnist David Grimes. He states my case much better than could I.

"Lassie, as you recall, was a collie with a high IQ. Unfortunately, she was stuck with a bunch of humans who had trouble putting their shoes on the right feet, let alone dealing with the rigors of life in the wilderness.

"It was a good thing the Martin family had Lassie around because otherwise they would have all been dead five minutes into the first show. Mr. Martin, who apparently had been kicked in the head by a horse at some early stage of his life, chose his family's home site on the basis of how many abandoned mine shafts there were in the area, and also on the number of mountain lions, which were thicker in those parts than med-flies in Bradenton.

"Timothy, who presumably had his umbilical cord knotted around his neck at birth, spent his childhood seeking out, and falling into, every abandoned mine shaft in the county. There was always a mountain lion in or near the mine shaft into which Timmy had fallen.

"Mrs. Martin spent the entire 20 year run of the show in the kitchen, stirring a pot of something or other. But she was the smartest one of the bunch. Sometimes it would take her only 15 or 20 minutes to figure out that Lassie's barks meant that Timmy had fallen down yet another mine shaft, and was in danger of drowning in the hysterical drool of laughing mountain lions."

DOGS HURT MY REPUTATION

"Once at a dinner party, I said I didn't like dogs," wrote Robert Fulghum in his book 'It Was On Fire When I Lay Down On It'. "The sudden silence made my ears ring. I could not have drawn more attention to myself if I had stood up on a chair and screamed 'I have rabies!' Some of the people present still give me a wide berth."

I can empathize with Fulghum. While I don't dislike dogs, I must confess to not being a dog lover. Because of this I've discovered that folks like me are often viewed in the same category as serial rapists and child molesters.

In newspaper columns I've written, I discovered it is safer to write about the shortcomings of spouses than those of dogs. I caught all kinds of hell about a dog column I wrote. This never happened when I wrote about spouses. Which leads me to the conclusion that people evidently like their dogs more than they do their mates.

I really don't feel that I am a bad person just because I don't love dogs. I hate to see any animal mistreated or hurt. I once even almost killed myself running off the road to keep from hitting a stupid rabbit. And I love children and don't beat my wife (but that may be because I'm afraid she'll hit me back.)

One of the reasons I'm sure is responsible for this lack of dog enthusiasm, was their proclivity to use my front yard as their latrine. Trying to mow the lawn, dodging dog piles, is never easy. I once counted exactly 55 of these piles I had to zigzag around. Even worse was raking leaves, because the piles are unseen under the leaves, causing me to step in them. Which I usually didn't discover until I had tracked particularly ripe dog poop into the house.

And I'm not real certain that dogs are always the great friends owners make them out to be. My friend Betty Kirkman fixed her dog's supper one evening, and headed outdoors to feed him. She tripped and fell awkwardly, badly breaking her leg in the process. As she lay there groaning in pain, did "man's best friend":

a.) Run to get help, a la Lassie? Or

b.) Try to console his mistress by showing his love and concern for her pain and suffering?

The answer is c.) Neither. Her "best friend" was too busy eating his supper off her chest where it had landed during the fall.

It always seemed to me that rather than "Dog is man's best friend", it is obvious that instead "Man is dog's best friend."

CUTESY GRANDPARENT NAMES

When I was a child, which was admittedly many moons ago, grandparents were called "Grandpa and Grandma". No longer is this the case. It seems that nowadays people vie for the cutest grandparental names.

No longer is "Granny" acceptable. Nowadays we have instead "Me-me's, Nana's, Me-moo's, Ma-moos, Me-ma's," etc. And instead of "Gramps" we have "Paw-paw", and probably "Hee-haw" for grandfathers who are jackasses. My six foot six friend Don Keiser is known as "Big" by his grandchildren . And I met a man at Disney World who was wearing a "Goofy" cap.

"Durned if I'd advertise that I'm goofy," I told him. "This cap was given to me by my granddaughter," he replied. "That's what all my grandchildren call me." Which I think is a great name for a grandparent.

I must admit to being a contributor to this dumb naming. When my first grandchild was born, there was the usual discussion about what we grandparents would be called. Our friends Mary and Rosy Hall's son, David, was stationed in Hawaii, where the name for grandmother was "Tutu." So my wife became "Tutu."

"That's okay," I unfortunately remarked, "as long as I'm not "Poopoo." So they of course then dubbed me "Pooh", which I bear to this day. That's bad enough, but then some of my friends who heard about it, started calling me " Doo-doo."

I'm a slow learner. As my granddaughters got older, I often signed missives and emails to them, "Dear Old Grandfather," which I at times shortened to the initials "DOG". It never dawned on me until now, that if anyone combines the two monickers, I become "Dog Pooh."

PEOPLE WHO GIVE BAD ADVICE

Much of this bum advice I've received, has been about investments. This has caused me to be one of those stupid investors whose results turn out to be, "Buy high, sell low," rather than the other way around

I'm ashamed to admit that at times I have also been guilty of giving bad advice at times.

"My new glasses you prescribed are fine," Mrs. Dowd told me when I was still practicing optometry. "But the Rx sunglasses don't seem right."

"You're right," I told her after checking them out. "The lab made one of the lenses wrong. I apologize for our not having caught the error. It was our responsibility to do so."

"No need to apologize. In fact I appreciate your honesty. Another doctor I went to recently made an obvious mistake, but never would admit it, and I lost all respect for him."

So I figured this was a great moral lesson about honesty, and wrote about it in my column "Lessons Learned" which appeared monthly in a national optometric journal. A few weeks later I received an email from one of the optometrist readers which stated:

"I followed your advice, and admitted a mistake I had made to one of our patients. Rather than thanking me for my honesty, she has sued me for malpractice."

MY LOUSY MEMORY

"Why are you crying, old man?" asked a bystander as an elderly gentleman sat on the curb, sobbing.

"I got married a few months ago to the most wonderful woman in the world. She's 50 years younger than I am, and gorgeous, but she loves me passionately, and takes wonderful care of me. In addition she's a marvelous cook."

"What then do you have to cry about?"

"Because I can't remember where I live!" he sobbed.

My memory hasn't gotten that bad as yet, but I find it becoming worse year by year. And it's a real pain, although there are some advantages in having a bad memory: You can put on your own Easter egg hunt. You only need two books in your library. You make new friends every day. Your secrets are safe with your friends because they can't remember them either. Etc. But they are counter-balanced by the embarrassments a bad memory can cause.

I was having lunch with an old friend, the late Dr. Bill Sullins.. He was telling me of some episode. With my old age hearing, I had to ask him to repeat it. With his old age memory he couldn't remember what he'd been talking about. A pretty good synopsis of the problems of old age.

But I'm happy to learn that memory problems have nothing to do with intelligence and happen even to smart people. I read that in his later years, Albert Einstein was riding a suburban train one day. The conductor came by to collect tickets, but Einstein couldn't find his.

"It's okay, Dr. Einstein," said the conductor. "A man of your eminence doesn't need to show me a ticket." Nevertheless, Einstein continued to search in his pockets for the ticket.

"You don't need to show me a ticket," again stated the conductor. "There is no need for you to continue looking for it."

"You don't understand," replied Einstein. "I have to find the ticket so I'll remember where I'm going."

Even love life can be affected by old age forgetfulness. An example is the elderly gentleman in a retirement home, who fell in love with another resident, and one evening asked her to marry him. But the next morning he couldn't remember whether she had said yes or no. Thus he had to phone her to find out.

"I apologize, but with my bad memory I can't remember what your answer was when I proposed to you last night," he told her.

"I said, 'Yes, yes, yes! And I meant it with all my heart!'" she replied.

"I am so glad. And again I apologize for my bad memory."

"No need to apologize," said she. "As a matter of fact, I appreciate you phoning, since I couldn't remember who it was that asked me."

One last example of the embarrassment old age memory can cause: "I'll bet you can't guess how old I am," a male nursing home resident said to a lady resident."

"If you'll drop your pants, I can tell you exactly how old you are," she replied. So he dropped his trousers, and she said, "You're 86."

"That's right!" he exclaimed. "How could you tell?"

"You told me yesterday, you old fool."

LOUD KIDS

You're on a plane. It's a long flight so you look forward to:

a.) Getting a lot of work done.
b.) Quietly reading a book.
c.) Catching up on your sleep.

Unfortunately, your seat mates are a momma and her small kid. The kid is wild and noisy, and makes your life miserable. The momma knows how cute the kid is, so is sure that you're enjoying the little darling, and does nothing to curb him. She would be horrified if she realized that you were seriously contemplating throttling her little darling.

I have a friend who didn't marry until he was 40. He was not used to having kids around, and his bride had two rambunctious boys, ages three and five. On their first vacation trip driving to Florida, they were making my friend crazy with their fighting and yelling in the back seat.

His rather drastic solution to the problem was to stop at the next town and trade his car for an SUV, in order to be able to separate them and get a little peace and quiet.

MALE CHAUVINISM

"Stand back," a man said to the lady who was bending over a man who had just fainted on the sidewalk. "I've had first aid training and I'll take care of this."

"Okay," said the lady. "And when you get to the part where you're supposed to call a doctor, I'll be right here."

In an attempt to get forgiven (particularly at home) for the kidding remarks I've made about women in general and wives in particular, I do hastily want to state that male chauvinism like this really does hack me. I often wonder how my Southern Baptist friends get away with their chauvinistic pronouncements about females.

"The Southern Baptist Convention, without debating the substance of the issue, went on record in opposition to ordination of women to the ministry," read a UPI news item. "Women's subservient role," it said, "is because of their responsibility for bringing sin into the world."

In my vast experience of living with womankind, four optometric assistants, four granddaughters, three daughters, and two wives (not concurrently of course) I've discovered among other things:

a.) The best way to make a female type person want to do something is to tell her she can't.

b.) Any mention of them having a subservient role is like waving a red flag in front of a bull.

c.) They don't even like to be blamed for leaving the bathroom light on, let alone all the sins of the world.

My other favorite story on the subject is about the man who asked for an appointment with a large law firm's best attorney. He was shown into their conference room, and when what he assumed was a secretary came in, he said to her, "Honey, how about running down to the drug store and bringing me a cup of coffee while I'm waiting." She returned 15 minutes later with the coffee.

"This coffee just cost you $101," she told him. "One dollar for the coffee, and $100 for my $400 an hour legal fee."

WIVES' IMPERFECTIONS

Columnist Art Buchwald once pointed out that it is the duty of all husbands to periodically point out the deficiencies of their wives in order to give them an opportunity to improve. However I have found that this sort of advice is not always appreciated. In fact, come to think of it, I can think of nary a time that such advice was received with jubilation.

Other husbands, braver than I, have pointed out imperfections of their wives:
- "We've been married 50 years. My wife is a good old gal, comfortable as an old shoe. But like an old shoe, every part of her is worn out except for the tongue."
- "My wife's cooking is so bad, the flies got together and mended the screen door."
- "I don't like the looks of your wife," the doctor told me after he had examined her. "I don't either, but she is good to the kids."
- "When your wife says she's nothing but a cook and a maid," said Comedian Alan King, " you can say, "That's not true! If you were only a cook and a maid, you'd have been fired a long time ago.'"
- Also from King is this advice. "When your wife says 'My mother warned me I shouldn't marry you!' the best reply is 'That's the only thing your mother and I have ever agreed on!'"
- "I'm lonely God," said Adam.

"Then I'll send you a companion named 'woman'," said God. "She will be a joy to you. She will take care of you, and cook for you, and obey your every word, and never, never, complain."

"That sounds great. But what will it cost me?"

"An arm, and a leg, and an eye," replied God.

"That's pretty expensive," said Adam. " What can I get for just a rib?"

MARTYRS

I do feel sorry for martyrs who are always complaining about the tough life they have. But at the same time I can't help but think of the story of the original Siamese Twins. I can think of no worse condition than existing while joined to another human being. Yet they adapted and lived a productive life, evidently without considering themselves martyrs.

I went to Kenya a number of years ago, and in our tour group was a man named Kester Sink, from Mt. Airy, NC, model for the town of Mayberry in the Andy Griffith TV show. His deceased wife was a granddaughter of one of the original Siamese twins, and he is living in the house built by her grandfather in 1844. He's the one who told me their story.

The twins were discovered in Siam by an American who brought them to the US at an early age. They were joined by a section of cartilage attached to both at the center of their chests. Even though this placed them in a facing position, they had learned to turn sideways sufficiently that they could face somewhat forward in walking. Their names were Eng and Chang. They were both very intelligent and their appearances across the country consisted of acrobatics and verbal discussion.

Tiring of constantly being on the road, they bought a farm near Mt. Airy, and married sisters. After a couple of years, they settled in separate houses, spending three days at one wife's house, and the next three at the other's. This seemed to work so well that over the next few years, between them they sired 21 children. It is mind boggling to picture how they accomplished this, but again rather than crying about their situation, they made the best of it.

WIFE INEFFICIENCY

I spent three years as a widower. First time in my life that I was King of the Castle and could do what I want. I could organize and do things as I wished for the first time in my life.

I discovered a number of time savers that made my life much easier and more efficient. For example, I found that keeping the cereal box on the kitchen table, rather than having to put it in the cupboard after every use, was a great time saver. I figured it took about 30 seconds to move it from the table to the cupboard following breakfast, and another 30 seconds to get it out the next morning.

Thus I was saving one minute a day---over the three year period that amounts to over 1,000 minutes, or about 17 hours of my valuable productive time. Similar time computations could also be made for such things as washing the dishes only after you run out of clean ones, rather than every day. And for not making the bed unless you are expecting company that will be inspecting your bedroom. There is no telling how many hours I saved from these and other behavioral modifications I made.

Alas. At the end of that three year period, I screwed the whole thing up by getting married again. I asked her if it was okay if I continued to keep the cereal box on the table.

"Of course," she replied enthusiastically. I was pleased with her understanding until she continued, "As long as you paint it to match the kitchen décor." I realized then, too late, that I was in trouble.

You will not be surprised to also learn that the bed is made more often now that I have a roommate. The other night, we were going out for the evening, leaving about 6:00 PM. "Are you ready?" I asked her. "Just a minute. I have to make the bed first," she replied!! No one was going to see it, even we! As soon as we got home, we'd be going to bed. Yet she just couldn't leave it unmade. Only thing I could figure was that in case of a robbery she wanted to make certain that the burglars would see that she kept a neat house. My research reveals that evidently most wives are this bad. Or even worse.

"My wife is such a neatnick," a friend told me, "that when I got up last night to go to the bathroom at 3:00 AM, when I returned to bed my wife had already made the bed."

In order to remove myself from the doghouse, I must interject that my new bride is a lovely and sweet lady, who I dearly love, and well worth all the inconveniences she causes! Even when I don't understand her.

WOMEN'S HOUSE DÉCOR

I can't help but notice that my household décor has changed drastically since my remarriage. Things are no longer the way I had them arranged.

One difference I find is that the towels and washcloths in my abode now always match. However I have also noted that they don't get me any cleaner or dryer that the mismatches I was formerly using. Window decorations are also not the same.

"Haven't you noticed how the new living room drapes pull the room together?" What's Her Name asked me after their installation. "Hell, I hadn't even noticed that it was falling apart," was my unfortunate rejoinder.

And our opinion of whether the house is clean is vastly different. As Dave Barry once wrote, "The primary difference between men and women is that women can see extremely small quantities of dirt, even at the molecule level. Men don't notice it until it forms clumps large enough to support agriculture."

The other main difference in the house is the proliferation of plant life. I've found that all womankind are not happy unless they have moved nature's greenery from outdoors to inside the house.

We have a sun porch. I have a chair in it in which I enjoy reading. Even though the room is quite small, I counted the other day and there are thirteen large plants of some sort in there. A couple of them are even trees! Every time I enter this sun porch to get to my chair, I feel as if I'm penetrating a jungle, and wishing I had a machete with me in order to hack my way through the foliage separating me from my chair.

It appears to me that if the good Lord had intended for plant life to be indoors rather than outdoors, he would have placed it there in the first place. What's Her Name obviously does not agree.

POLITICAL CORRECTNESS

There's a lady optometrist at the University of California Medical Center who does not look on me with kindly benevolence. She has never met me personally; otherwise I'm certain she would be impressed with my personal charm.

The reason for her lack of enthusiasm for me is a story I told in a column for a national optometric journal. I was attempting to make the point that everyone has good qualities, if you'll but search for them. I thought the story made the point and was also right funny—she thought it was chauvinistic and evidently didn't see any hilarity in it.

The story was the old one about the 12 year old boy who was sent to dancing class by his parents, much against his will. To make matters worse, he was assigned the least desirable girl in the class as his dancing partner. She was sarcastic, loud mouthed, homely, and outweighed him by a good 60 pounds. She also was a lousy dancer and had an unfortunate tendency to spend a good percentage of the time tromping on his feet.

"You must also learn the social graces," said the teacher to the boys in the class. "I want each of you to compliment your partner in some way when you finish dancing with her."

"Whatever can I find to compliment about this girl?" asked the lad of himself as he again winced from having his toes trod upon for the umpteenth time. But finally came an inspiration, and at the completion of the dance, he gallantly said to her, "You sweat less than any fat girl I ever danced with!"

After this appeared in print I soon received the following "fan letter" from the aforementioned lady:

"I assume you are unaware of the presence of women practicing optometry. In your recent column, the perspiring obese dance neither amused nor instructed me."

Too many people nowadays have lost their sense of humor, and react to kidding as a "put down". When I was a mere lad and became upset one day at being teased by a schoolmate, my father gave me a sage bit of advice I've always remembered:

"You should take kidding as a compliment rather than getting upset about it. People kid only folks they like. Haven't you noticed that if you don't like someone, you ignore and stay away from him, rather than kidding him?"

Comedian Jackie Mason once also lamented the fact that it was no longer possible to kid any ethnic group. "The only nationality you can kid any more is the Irish," he said. "And that's only because they're too drunk to notice it."

However it appears to me that people of Scottish Ancestry seem to handle pretty well the kidding they take about being overly thrifty. For example:

Angus McTavish had died, and his widow wanted to announce the fact in the local newspaper. However, she had heard that the paper charged ten cents per word, so kept it as short as possible, "Angus McTavish died." The editor phoned her to tell her that she could use three additional words at no extra cost.

"Okay," she responded. "Just add 'Oldsmobile for sale'."

BEING A JOB REFERENCE

I hate to receive job reference forms. I never know what to say. So I decided once to just wing it with my answers, when I received such a form for a friend who was applying for a job:

Q. Age?

A. He CLAIMS he is 45.

Q. Sex?

A. Possibly. However if he is fooling around, his wife doesn't know about it.

Q. Religion?

A. Presbyterian. However, luckily for them, he never attends church.

Q. How long have you known applicant?

A. Too long

Q. Is he civic minded?

A. Yes. He gave a dollar to the United Fund last year.

Q. Is he thrifty?

A. More like "cheap".

Q. If you had an opening would you hire this person for your company?

A. I'll try to think of a kind answer as soon as I can stop laughing.

Q. Is he industrious?

A. He's not afraid of work. He can lie down and go to sleep right next to it.

Q. Do you think he is well suited for this job?
A. Yes.
Q. Why?
A. He's tried just about every other type of job and failed. Thus it is obvious by the process of elimination that this HAS to be what he's suited for.

Incidentally, he got the job. Which shows how much influence I have.

TEACHING A WIFE TO DRIVE

I read somewhere that divorce was much more prevalent in the 20th Century than it was in the 19th. That sound plausible. The automobile hadn't been as yet invented in the 19th Century. Teaching a wife to drive a mule had to cause a whole lot less argument, than teaching her to drive an automobile.

In 1946 I was fresh out of the Navy, and back in optometry school in Memphis with a newly acquired wife. The G.I. Bill was paying my school expenses. My bride had a job that paid the rent and put food on the table. Between the two I was being supported adequately if not luxuriously.

In fact, by 1947 we were able to dig up 500 bucks to purchase a 1937 Chrysler Royal with Free Wheeling. Since the brakes didn't work half the time, it was REALLY free wheeling. Since my bride was supporting me, I figured I'd reciprocate by teaching her to drive.

Somehow the marriage survived this experience. "Don't watch me, it makes me nervous," she'd say. So I'd close my eyes, which was the best way to put up with her driving anyway.

"What did I do wrong?" she'd ask as the car would jump, stall, and end up over the curb. "How can I tell if you won't let me watch you?" I'd reply, a trace of hysteria creeping into my voice.

One Saturday night she was driving us to a friend's house. The route took us through the main intersection at Crump Stadium at the precise time 25,000 people were arriving for a football game. She panicked and stalled the car right smack in the middle of the intersection, completely blocking traffic from all four directions.

The cacophony of horns, and "gentle" words of advice from her husband created still more panic, and she couldn't get the car started again. Without saying a word, she got out of the car, and climbed into the back seat. Thus it was left to me to take over the controls and absorb the dirty looks, shouting, and honking from impatient motorists, as I unsuccessfully attempted to start the flooded engine. The whole experience was so stressful that I have absolutely no recollection of how we finally got out of there.

Her unfortunate tendency to "desert the ship" in times of crisis continued after we and the Chrysler moved to Rome, GA. "Mary asked me to call and tell you the car is stalled in the middle of the South Broad (two lane) Bridge," a friend phoned me during a busy day at my office. "She got a ride home and wants you to go get the car."

Two weeks later the brakes again gave way, and I again received a call at the office requesting that I come rescue the car, which was perched half way over a ten foot embankment. Being a fairly lucid person, I realized a turning point had arrived in my life, and I was going to have to either:

(a). Get rid of the car, or

(b). Get rid of the wife

Some quick mental arithmetic convinced me that (a) would be a helluva lot cheaper than (b). So I traded the car.

Another problem concerned with autos that causes marital discord is back seat driving. I read somewhere of the man who cured his wife of this fault. He had the steering wheel loosened and an attachment added to the steering column that allowed him to steer with his knees.

The next day they were doing 65 MPH on a crowded freeway. His wife was doing her customary job of backseat driving. "If you don't like the way I drive," he screamed, "then YOU drive!" With that, he removed the steering wheel from the column and handed it to her.

Reportedly, she fainted.

YANKEE CRITICS

"I'm 'repairin' to go to town," a native Georgian told his Yankee friend.

"You mean 'preparing'," responded the Yankee. "Repairing means 'to fix'."

"That's what I said. I'm 'fixin' to go to town."

I must confess that many years ago I would have been just as confused. I was then a Yankee before I got wiser (and colder) and moved to Georgia. I have come to enjoy the colorful, melodic, and friendly Southern accent and idiom, and now become irritated when Yankees make fun of it.

In addition to 'fixin', there were other terms that were perplexing to me at first:

Summers---"I know that boy is around here summers"

War—"Be careful. Don't get stuck on that barb war."

Tarred—"I'm too tarred to go out tonight.

Tar arn—"You can't fix a flat tire without a tar arn."

Ratcheer—"I left my keys ratcheer, and now they're gone."

Airs—"That shortstop done made two airs already."

What Yankees don't realize is that talkin' Southern doesn't take nearly as much effort because it often reduces the number of syllables in a word or phrase:

Cain't—can-not
Jev-ver—did you ev-er
Co-col-a—co-ca-co-la
Nome—No ma'am
Zackly---exactly
Cyst—assist
Prolly—probably

And the one syllable "y'all" is surely much easier to say than "all of you." The two prize winners, however, are one syllable words that replace four syllables:

Spear—su-per-i-or
Nairn—nar-y a one.

However, I must admit one thing still baffles me. When so many Southern words efficiently reduce the number of syllables, I can't understand why a few instead add a syllable.

Damn—"Frankly my dear, I don't give a 'day-um'."
Grits—"I had gri-yuts for breakfast."
Fan—"It was so hot, I had to turn on the fay-un."

But another efficiency of Southernese, is that you can often use the same pronunciation for more than one word. For example on the old Candid Camera TV show, I heard the announcer ask a gentleman from South Carolina, "How do you pronounce the word spelled f-a-r?"

"Fahr," he replied.

"How do you pronounce the word spelled f-i-r-e?"

"Fahr," was again the response.

"Then those two words are pronounced just the same?"

"No, no, no!!" he responded fervently. "F-a-r- is pronounced 'fahr', and f-i-r-e is pronounced 'fahr'."

LIFE ISN'T FAIR

Some of comedian Steven Wright's one liners illustrate the fact that life is not always fair:
- If everything seems to be going well, you have overlooked something.
- When everything is coming your way, you're in the wrong lane.
- The early bird may get the worm, but it's the second mouse that gets the cheese.
- If you want the rainbow, you gotta put up with the rain.
- Eagles may soar, but weasels don't get sucked into jet engines.

Doing the right thing seems to seldom pay off with tangible rewards. I was once playing golf with the late Bill Buchanan when I hit my drive out of bounds. Nice guy that he was, Bill went into the woods to retrieve my ball for me. His reward for this kind and thoughtful act? While he was in there, a bird on a limb above him splattered him right on top of his head.

Which reminds me of a Born Loser comic strip that I put on my refrigerator, because I thought it taught a great lesson about how life is not always fair. In the strip, the Born Loser was walking down the street in the first panel. The second panel shows him being "splattered" by a bird on the tree limb above. In the third panel he is gazing skyward, and saying to the bird, "For everyone else, you sing!"

Another example of how good deeds often go unappreciated: A lady was first in line at a crowded bus stop as the bus pulled up. As she tried to step up to the first step, she discovered that the tight skirt she was wearing would not allow her to raise her leg sufficiently to make the step. People were crowding in behind her, and yelling at her to hurry up and get on the bus.

Finally, in desperation, she reached around behind her and partially unzipped her skirt, in hopes that would loosen it enough to enable her to make the step. Still she couldn't raise her leg sufficiently to do so. With that, the man behind her solved her problem by clasping her around the waist and lifting her to the top of the step. Then he followed and took her in his arms and kissed her. Rather than thanking him, she instead slapped his face and said:

"Just because you helped me board the bus doesn't mean that you, a complete stranger, can take such liberties!"

"Well, Lady," he replied. "I thought we'd become pretty good friends, after you unzipped my trousers back there."

Which proves the old adage, "No good deed goes unpunished."

"The secret of life can be summed up in five words," once said Aldous Huxley. "You get used to it."

NO SYMPATHY

I once had surgery on a very unglamorous region of my anatomy, one that looks to the south when one is facing north. From this experience I learned that your friends(?) will not always show proper sympathy for your pain and suffering.

Our church has a men's prayer breakfast once a week. One of its functions is to pray for those who are sick, suffering, and infirm. Which is certainly what I was prior to and immediately following my hemorrhoid operation that had taken place the day before.

But when the group discovered the region of my surgery, the most prevalent reaction was one of laughter and levity, rather than prayer for my recovery or relief from the pain. A dentist friend, Dr. Burr Ward, even had effrontery to say, "If that's the region of his anatomy they're operating on, there probably won't be anything left of him after the surgery."

"You always were a pain in the butt," was as close as I got to compassion from other friends. And even Dr. Bob Allred, my preacher, joined the levity. He phoned when I was still in the hospital to tell me he was coming to see me that afternoon.

"I won't be here. I'm being discharged at noon," I told him. "That's a relief," he chortled. "I heard the region of your surgery and I was afraid you might ask for a laying on of hands."

Prior to surgery I kept painfully limping to the office of my good friend and golfing buddy, Dr. John Dickinson. I thought he had lost his mind, because he seemingly had forgotten my name and called me "Ben Dover" rather than "Jack Runninger." Until I realized that he was not calling me by that name, but instead was giving me a command for the position I was to assume for the examination.

When it was agreed surgery was the only course for relief, I was resigned and ready. Until the morning of the surgery, when the following thought occurred to me:

"Do you realize," I said to myself, "that this John Dickinson, the surgeon who is about to slice on your anatomy with what you hope is a reasonable degree of accuracy, is the same guy who can't sink a 12 inch putt?!" Fortunately, I discovered he was a better surgeon than golfer.

When I was served breakfast in the hospital, I was reminded of an acquaintance's hospital experience. A glass of apple juice was on his breakfast tray. Since he didn't want it, he poured the juice in the urinalysis bottle, so he could use the glass for water.

When the nurse came in a few minutes later, he noticed her looking with suspicion at the liquid in the urinalysis bottle.

"It does look a little cloudy, doesn't it. Perhaps it will clear up if I run it through again," he said as he grasped the urinalysis bottle and drank its contents. Reportedly the nurse fainted.

GRADUATIONS

"We are gathered here today," wrote humorist Dave Barry, "you, the eager members of the class of 2004, and we, your family members, who will sit on hard folding chairs until every last eager one of you has picked up a diploma, at which point we will feel as though the entire Riverdance troupe has been stomping on our buttocks.

"Because, gosh, there sure are a lot of you in the Class of 2004, and we are fighting to stay awake."

I found myself empathizing with him as I attended my granddaughters high school commencement exercises. Seeing her receive her diploma was a very pleasurable 30 seconds. It was the other hour and a half that was hellacious.

"There's gotta be a better system," I said to myself as my buttocks grew increasingly paralyzed from sitting on the hard bleacher seats, and realized that we had barely gotten part way through the D's. It was going to be a long time before we reached the W's and my granddaughter.

As my mind wandered, it occurred to me that in the future perhaps we could combine commencement with an athletic event. Each of the grads would be timed on how quickly they could run up to the stage, grab their diploma and get back to their seat. The winner would be declared co-valedictorian. This would speed things up considerably.

The only exception would be when it came your granddaughter's turn. She would be granted plenty of time to walk gracefully across the stage, and perhaps even given the opportunity to make a short speech detailing how she owed her success and good looks to her grandfather.

My thoughts wandered to my high school graduation many moons ago. For some strange reason, I had been asked to give a talk on our relations with Canada. What that had to do with high school graduation, I have no idea. At my age of failing memory, I have difficulty remembering what I ate for breakfast. Yet still etched on my mind almost 70 years later are the opening words of my speech:

"Although Canada is our nearest neighbor and the third largest county in world, there are few countries about which Americans know less. To most Americans, Canada is populated mainly by the Dionne quintuplets and the Northwest Mounted Police......"

How does that grab you? Think about the poor families sitting on hard bleachers having to endure this (and two other similar speeches) before they could watch 320 graduates slowly march across the stage to receive their diplomas.

I think Barry probably has the best solution. He said next time he had a child graduating, he was going to rename him Aaron A. Aardvark so that he would be the first one to receive a diploma. His family could then leave the building and go to lunch.

OBSERVANT PEOPLE

What's Her Name can spot a tiny spot on my shirt or tie from a distance of three and a half miles. This makes it uncomfortable for me while eating, since I am basically a slob.

(I'm not quite as bad as the guy who was told by a lady, "You're so slovenly it's disgusting. I can even tell that you had eggs for breakfast because you haven't washed your face.

"You're wrong, Lady," he replied. "I had cereal this morning. It was yesterday I had eggs.")

Another observant person: "I'll bet I can tell where you went to college," said one cocktail party participant to another. "I doubt it," said the other gentleman. "you've only known me since we met five minutes ago at this party."

"Nevertheless, I think you're a Harvard graduate."

"You're very observant! I am a Harvard grad. How could you tell?"

"Your obvious culture and good breeding, impeccable tailoring, excellent vocabulary, New England accent, and gentlemanly manner all led me to this conclusion."

"If you're so durned observant and smart," said another man in the conversational group, "where did I go to college?"

"You went to the University of Alabama."

"That's right!. How could you tell?"

"I saw your school ring when you were picking your nose."

Some folks aren't that observant. "I can't get that cute new guy to notice me," complained an elderly lady in a retirement home.

"I know what you can do to get him to notice you," said a friend. "Take off all your clothes and streak past his doorway." Which she proceeded to do.

"My eyes ain't what they used to be," the elderly gentleman said to his equally elderly friend. "Can you tell what that lady who just ran past our door was wearing."

"Nope," replied the friend. "But whatever it was, it sure did need ironing."

COMMUNICATING WITH KIDS

When Dr. Donald Bennett was a small child, he would often go to the grocery store with his mother Trude. He was extremely proud of his father, so when strangers would ask him, "Who are you, young man?", he would proudly reply, "I'm Dr. Irving Bennett's son!"

"I know you're proud of your daddy," Trude said to him one day. "But I think it would be better in the future if you just say, 'I'm Donald Bennett,' when someone asks who you are."

The very next day they were back at the store, and sure enough, another shopper asked him, "Who are you young man?" Obediently, he replied, "I'm Donald Bennett."

"Oh, are you Dr. Irving Bennett's son?" asked the lady.

"I always thought so, but Momma says no."

Communicating with children is often frustrating, due to their lack of experiential background, and thus meanings of words. One of the most heart tugging examples of this was told to me by a friend in St. Louis.

A five year old neighbor of his fell off his bicycle and broke his jaw. When they took him to the emergency room, the doctor told them, "We're going to have to put him to sleep in order to set the jaw."

The boy when he heard this went to pieces. He cried and cried, and could not be consoled. Eventually his parents discovered the problem. The boy's interpretation of being put to sleep was what they had had to do to their dog a few weeks earlier.

NOT LISTENING

After all, what I have to say is a lot more important than what you want to say. So it pisses me off when you obviously aren't listening to me, or even worse, interrupt me.

I'm certain the same thing has happened to you---often! I hate it when it happens to me. The problem is that I have a tendency to do the same dang thing. I thought I'd learned my lesson more than 50 years ago, but I keep forgetting it.

I had just graduated from optometry school and was establishing my practice in Rome, GA. I was desperately trying to keep the wolf away from my door by attracting patients to seek my services. The very first day after I had started, I went to the Busy Bee for lunch after a tiring morning of doing zilch. I was seated at a table next to a gentleman named Fred Stivers. He was the superintendent of Southeastern Mills, the makers of Stivers Best Flour, and obviously an important citizen.

"Aha," I said to myself. "This is a perfect opportunity to impress this influential man by telling him about how well trained I am, and what a great optometrist I am." I decided it might be a little rude to hit him with both barrels early in our conversation, so I figured I'd ask him a couple of questions about his work, and then smoothly turn the conversation to me.

Only problem was that I got so interested in what he told me about the milling of flour, that I kept asking questions. Lo and behold, by the time I was ready to turn the conversation to me and my occupation, it was too late---the lunch hour was over. As we left the restaurant, I cussed myself for having missed such a great opportunity to impress him about my new practice.

A few days later, he phoned my office to make an appointment for him and for his wife. It dawned on me that once again I had been smarter by accident than I am by intent. I had impressed him a whole lot more by listening to him, rather than trying to get him to listen to me. Great lesson. But I keep forgetting it.

You communicate better with others when you listen. The dictionary defines communication as to give AND to receive information. We communicate WITH other folks, not TO them.

One of the problems is that it's difficult to keep paying attention. The average speaking rate is 125 words per minute, while the average listening rate is 400—600 words a minute   Thus it's hard to keep your mind on what's being said. And you misunderstand if you don't pay attention.

"Listening" or paying attention is also important with the written word as well as the spoken word, if you want to get the correct message. One of the questions on a government survey about small business employees, read, "How many employees do you have, broken down by sex."

"None that I know of," wrote the small business owner. "Our chief problem is alcohol."

BEING A NUMBER

Do you feel sometimes in this modern world you're becoming a number rather than a person? We don't seem to be identified by name anymore, but rather by Social Security number, tax ID number, bank account number, credit account number, pin number, password, health insurance policy number, credit card number, etc.

The late Sam Levenson said we may soon be identified on our tombstones in the following manner:

Here
To the best of
Our knowledge
Lies
017534985470836
Hatched 1940
Matched 1965
Dispatched 2010

Come to think of it, it might be helpful if everyone did become a specific number, which could then be stenciled on their foreheads. It would eliminate the necessity of trying to remember names, which has always been a problem for me. I'm not alone in that weakness.

Many years ago, whenever I purchased something at Huff Pharmacy, Bobby Huff would call me Randy. After this had been going on for two years, one day he apologized for having had me mixed up with Randy Green. When I got home and looked at the sales slip, I found he now had me identified as Bob Powell.

While on the subject of names, I do have a suggestion for all prospective parents, based on personal experience. If you plan to call your child "Bonzo," then for heaven's sake make that his official name, rather than using it as a nickname, and making his official name something like "Heathcliff Farquardt." It will save a great deal of confusion later in life.

I was named William John for my two grandfathers, William Runninger and John Grossman. But then my parents decided to call me Jack as a nickname for John, and I have gone through life as Jack Runninger. This may be what has warped my personality. On some documents I am Jack, and on others I am William John, which often creates confusion. And think of how much worse it would be if my last name was Smith.

Someone once gave me a jacket with the initials WJR embroidered on it. When folks who knew me as Jack asked about it, I tried to convince them it stood for "Wonderful Jack Runninger." However my granddaughters spoiled this when they decided it instead stood for "Weird Jack Runninger."

NON-COMMUNICATIVE COMMUNICATION

"Once upon a point in time, a small person named Little Red Riding Hood initiated plans for the preparation, delivery, and transportation of foodstuffs to her grandmother, a senior citizen residing at a place of residence in a wooded area of indeterminate dimension.

"In the process of implementing this program, her incursion into the area was in mid-transportation process when it attained interface with an alleged perpetrator. This individual, a wolf............."

This is the beginning of Russell Baker's translation of Little Red Riding Hood in his book, "So This Is Depravity," as an illustration of the distressing growing tendency for folks not to talk in plain English anymore. To illustrate it further, he told of hearing a radio announcer interviewing a physician ask him the purpose of his work.

"To facilitate patients' re-entry into society as functioning members," said the doctor.

"Why couldn't he have just said, "To get patients out of the hospital and back home?" lamented Baker.

I get the feeling that people nowadays are more concerned with showing the depth of their intellect rather than with making their message understandable. For example, I once heard on a TV news report, a fire department spokesperson said they had trouble investigating a plane crash due to the "nonpresence of any particular illumination." Seems like it would have been much easier and clearer to just say it was dark.

And when police detectives are interviewed about a robbery, why don't they ever say, "We caught the sucker who did it." Instead have you noticed that almost invariably they say, "The alleged perpetrator has been apprehended."

My all-time favorite came in a Rome (GA) News-Tribune article about the discovery of a severed head in a Tennessee lake. The Walker County sheriff was quoted as saying, "There is the strong probability that foul play is involved in this case."

Probability?! Perhaps they hadn't completely ruled out the possibility that the man's razor slipped while he was shaving?

Also I find that I am irked with "cutesy" condensations of words. Such as, "It was one of his very faves (favorites)," and "It was an absolutely fab (fabulous) affair." This practice gives me a a very large pain in my pos (posterior).

MY INVESTING STUPIDITY

"Business sure has been bad lately," complained haberdasher Lorden Taylor. "I sold only one suit on Tuesday, didn't sell anything on Wednesday, and Thursday was even worse!"

"How could Thursday be worse if you didn't sell anything on Wednesday?" I asked him.

"The guy that bought the suit Tuesday brought it back."

It comes as no news to you that the economy has been bad. "Has the fallen stock market caused you to lose sleep?" I asked a friend who I knew had most of his retirement funds in stocks. "I sleep like a baby," he replied.

"Really?" I said, unbelievingly.

"Yep. I wake up every couple of hours and cry."

There are now some new definitions for investment terms:

- Bull market—A random market movement causing an investor to mistake himself for a financial genius.
- P/E ratio—The percentage of investors wetting their pants as the market goes down.
- Standard and Poor—Your life in a nutshell.
- Cash Flow---The movement your money makes as it disappears down the toilet.

However I cannot place all the blame for my investment failures on the falling market. I was always a lousy investor even when times were good.

"Making money in the stock market is easy," was the tongue-in-cheek advice Bernard Baruch once gave. "All you have to do is buy stock at its lowest point, and sell it at its highest." Instead I seemed to develop an unerring ability to "buy high and sell low."

During my Navy days in World War II, I developed a close friendship with a guy I'll call Les Scruples to protect the guilty. I lost track of him after the war, until later when I read an article about him in Time Magazine. It identified him as one of the leading patent attorneys in the United States.

I contacted him and we re-established our friendship. I was undoubtedly dazzled by his big-wheel activities, and vacation home we visited in Key Biscayne, FL. So when he offered to let me in on a silver mine venture he was undertaking in Arizona, I borrowed money and became a minor miner.

Too late I discovered he had become an alcoholic, and my money now lies buried in the depths of the mine.

Still not convinced of my inadequacy as a financial genius, I next invested in a resort hotel that was being constructed. I watched them digging what I thought was the foundation for the building, only to later discover they were instead digging a grave for my money.

I may not be the brightest star in the firmament, but a few more such escapades finally convinced me I was not a financial genius, and I rejected all such future proposals.

Including a couple that turned out to be veritable gold mines.

BEING A LOUSY ENTREPRENEUR

"This is a 'must read' story that will really touch your heart," an idiot friend recently emailed me. It went like this:

One day a construction crew turned up to start building a house. The six year old daughter of the family next door started hanging out with the workers. The construction crew---gems in the rough---adopted her as a project mascot. They let her sit with them for coffee and lunch breaks, and gave her little jobs to do to make her feel important.

At the end of the week, they even presented her with a pay envelope containing a dollar. The little girl excitedly took the dollar home to her mother, who suggested they go to the bank and open a savings account.

"Where did you get the dollar?" asked the bank president.

"It's my pay for working with some men building a house all week," she proudly replied.

"Will you be working on the house again this week?"

"I will if those #%$&*@%'s at the lumberyard, ever bring us the $@% &*%& lumber," answered the little girl.

The little girl's financial success reminded me of the mind-warping entrepreneurial failures I have suffered all my life. My father was a school teacher who was never very happy with the remuneration his profession afforded him. Therefore he decided his #1 son (namely me) should early learn the attribures of a successful businessman, so that I could one day achieve the financial success that had eluded him.

His first effort came when I was ten years old, during the height of the depression. To develop my salesmanship skills, he had me selling magazines door to door. They sold for ten cents, and for each one I sold I received a commission of two cents. After three days, I had earned a total of eight cents. 75% of this sum came the day I took my cute four-year old brother with me and let him ask the question, "Do you wanna buy a 'mazzanine?"

My old man recognized that this enterprise was not developing the skills in his offspring he had hoped. However, he was persistent. He came to the erroneous conclusion that the problem was not in the peddler, but instead in the product being peddled. So when we visited farmer relatives, he purchased 20 dozen eggs for me to peddle door to door, pulling them behind me in my wagon.

At this undertaking I was numerically more successful. As I recall, I was able to sell about six dozen. The remainder was about evenly divided between those that got broken and those that became rotten before I got them peddled. The final accounting pretty well cancelled the eight cent profit I had made in the magazine business.

My sire finally recognized that he was probably going to go broke if he continued to finance my entrepreneurial enterprises. From then on he steered me instead into salaried positions such as mowing lawns, caddying, working in a grocery store, etc.

However he had evidently implanted the entrepreneurial spirit in me, so when I went off to college I searched for easy ways to make money to help pay college expenses. Thus I was easy prey for the fraternity brother who sold me the house laundry concession for 150 bucks.

"You'll make good money and then, when you are a senior, you can get the 150 bucks back by selling the concession to an incoming freshman," he assured me.

Two months later, Pearl Harbor came along, and soon most of us went off to war. So my laundry investment of course became worthless.

The fraternity house candy-bar concession was another one of my college business attempts. Gross sales were extremely successful, as the candy sold like hot cakes. Only problem was that I discovered the reason for the brisk sales was that the machine was offering a great bargain to its purchasers. For every nickel placed in the (candy bars only cost a nickel back then), the machine was delivering not only the candy bar of choice, but also refunding the nickel along with it.

All of this may have been the most important lesson I learned in college, since it evermore cured me of attempting further entrepreneurial attempts.

QUICK THINKERS

I have an unfortunate tendency for my mouth to often become operative prior to my brain doing so. In that way I am much like the gentleman who was cheating on his wife.

"What time is it?" he asked his paramour one evening while they were in bed together.

"It's 10:00," she replied.

"I've got to get home right away so my wife won't be suspicious." So he hurriedly dressed in the dark, and got home just as his wife was getting ready for bed.

"Where are your undershorts?" she asked him as he took off his pants preparing for bed. When he looked down he was horrified to discover that in his haste to get dressed in the dark, he had forgotten to don his shorts. Mouth operating before brain, he replied:

"Mygawd, I've been robbed!"

My inablility to think quickly is the reason I resent quick thinkers like the grocery clerk I heard about. A lady asked him if she could buy half a head of lettuce.

"Gee, I'll have to ask the manager," said he as he walked to the back of the store to find the manager.

"Some idiot wants to buy half a head of lettuce," he said to the manager. Then as he glanced around he found that the lady had followed him in his quest for the manager, and heard every word he said.

"But that's okay," he smoothly and immediately added. "This nice lady would like to purchase the other half."

Unfortunately I discovered that my friend noted educator Dr. Dave McCorkle also is at times a quick thinker. I had shamelessly boasted to him one day that my newspaper column had received the third place award in the National Newspaper Association' Better Newspaper Contest. He had a quick, and clever, response.

"It could be kind of like the story about the lady who thought she was a great cook, whereas in reality she was terrible. She baked a cake and entered it at the County Fair, and was excited when it was given the third place award.

"Until she learned that her cake was the only entry in the contest."

UNDERSTANDING ENGLISH LANGUAGE

Methodist preacher Larry Caywood was worried about the morals of one of the young women in his congregation. So when he met her on the street one day, he said to her, "Miss Jones, I want you to know I prayed for you three times last night."

"That wasn't necessary Preacher," she coyly replied. "All you had to do was call, and I'd have come right over."

It sort of exasperates me that the English language can often be interpreted in more ways than one. Another example is that of the six year old little hellion who was in first grade.

"Johnny is trying," read the note on his first report card. His parents were pleased, because he sure hadn't shown that tendency at home.

"Johnny is still trying," read the note on his second report card. Again his parents were pleased. Until the third report card note read:

"Johnny is still VERY trying."

My friend Dr. Jerry Parks from Arkansas was once worried about whether patients thought they had to wait too long for him to see them, when they came to his office. Thus he asking a lady patient one day, "What is your usual wait when you come to our office?" She looked at him with a puzzled expression for a few seconds, and then said, "About 155 pounds," with a "Why in hell are you asked me my weight?" on her face.

Another difficulty is that putting pauses at the wrong place in oral communication can completely change their meanings. At a church board meeting I attended, a lady made an announcement about the next meeting of her circle, which met at night since its members worked during the daytime.

"The ladies (pause)of the night circle, will meet next Thursday," was what she meant to convey. Unfortunately she got the pause in the wrong place, so what came out was, "The ladies of the night (pause) circle......"

"I think it's great that we are taking on a new ministry," I couldn't resist commenting to the board. "However I didn't realize that we had that many "ladies of the night" in our church. I thought it was funny. She didn't.

I can't remember the author's name, but I can never forget the title of her book, "Eats, Shoots, and Leaves." In it she tells of the Panda who walked into a bar, ordered a sandwich, pulled out a pistol and shot it, and then walked out.

"Why did you do that?" someone asked him.

"Look Panda up in the dictionary," he replied. So the person did so, and found the description of the Panda's diet, "Eats shoots and leaves."

Other examples from her book:

"The pickled herring merchant." A merchant who sells pickled herring?

Or a herring merchant who has been imbibing too freely?

"Leonora walked on her head, a little higher than usual." I guess you would have to be a little high to walk around on your head. Or try reading it instead with the comma moved forward to between "on" and "her".

"We had a reservation for the honeymoon suite at a fancy new hotel on our wedding night," the recent bride told a friend, begins one of my favorite examples of dual meanings of words. "It was a fiasco," she went on. "The hotel was so new the room wasn't yet completely furnished, and did not have a bed or a couch."

"What was your reaction?" asked the friend.
"I was floored!"

PEOPLE WHO ARE TOO AGREEABLE

Overall I of course prefer folks who are agreeable and pleasant. However, some overdo it, and I get the feeling they're not sincere nor honest in what they're saying. For example the conversation between two rural men who had not seen each other in awhile, and ran into each other in town one Saturday.

"What have you been doing?" said one.
"Wal, I got married," said the other.
"That's good."
"Wal, it ain't too good. She's awful ugly."
"That's too bad."
"Wal, it ain't too bad. She's got an awful lot of money."
"That's good."
"Wal, it ain't too good. She's awful stingy."
"That's too bad."
"Wal, it ain't too bad. She did buy me a house."
"That's good."
"Wal, it ain't too good. It done burned down."
"That's too bad."
"Wal, it ain't too bad. She were in it."

Incidentally, this story is an excellent example of the statement, "There are no new jokes." I discovered a version of this same story that appeared in 1693 in a book entitled "English Jests Refin'd and Improv'd."

Two persons who had been formerly acquainted, but had not seen each other a great while, meeting on the Road, one ask'd the other how he did; he told him he was very well, and was Married since he saw him: the other reply'd That was well indeed: not so well neither, said he, for I have Married a Shrew. That's ill, said the other. Not so ill neither, said he, for I had 2000 Pounds with her. That's well again, said his Friend. Not so well neither, for I laid it out in Sheep, and they died of the Rot. That was ill indeed, said the other. Not so ill neither, said he, for I sold the Skins for more money than the Sheep cost. That was well, indeed quoth his friend. Not so well neither, said he, for I laid out my money in a House and it was burned. That's very ill, said the other. Not ill neither , said he, *for my Wife was burned in it.*

PEOPLE WHO DON'T SHOW APPRECIATION

Like the elderly gentleman who was sitting in the living room by the fire, while his wife of 50 years sat across from him, knitting. To himself he mused, "You know, she has been a good wife all these years. She has cooked for me, mended my clothes, kept the house straight, did my laundry, and never complained.

"Yet I never took her anyplace, or remembered her birthday and our anniversary, or paid any attention to her, or ever thanked her for all she does. I guess it's time that I should tell her that I do appreciate her."

"Mandy, " he said aloud, "I'm proud of you!"

Mandy, who was a little hard of hearing, without looking up from her knitting, replied, "I'm tired of you too!!"

I AIN'T AS PURTY AS I USED TO BE

One of the things we have to put up with in our old age is that we don't look as good as we did when we were younger. Often we don't realize it because the change is so gradual, as we look in the mirror every morning over the years. Consequently contemporarily aged folks we see after a long time, always look so much older.

They tell the story of the 60 year old lady who went to see a Dr. Smiley, a dentist she had not visited before. When she first saw him, she thought, "He looks a little bit like Ben Smiley, who was in my high school class. But it couldn't be him, because he looks way too old to have been my classmate."

"Did you attend Bardwell High School?" she nevertheless asked him in order to make certain.

"Why, yes," he replied.

"You were in my class there!" she admitted.

"Really?" he responded. "What subject did you teach?"

My friend Dr. Bill Baldwin once went to his wife's 35th high school reunion. There is nothing worse than going to a spouse's reunion, because she sees all these old friends, while you know no one. Bill was standing next to another spouse, as they observed all the class grads greet each other after not having seen each other for 35 years.

"You haven't changed a bit since we graduated!" was the universal greeting.

The other spouse leaned over to Bill and whispered, "If none of these folks have changed a bit since they graduated, that had to be the crummiest looking class in the history of the school!"

Another good example of our loss of beauty took place in a retirement home. A new man had moved into the home, and immediately caught the attention of one of the widows.

"That new man is so cute, but I can't get him to notice me," she complained to a friend.

"I know how you can get him to notice you. Just take off all your clothes and 'streak' past his doorway in the nude."

So that's what she did. Another resident was in his room with him when the 'streaking' occurred. He asked, "Did you see that lady who ran by the door? Could you see what she was wearing?"

"Nope," replied the other. "But whatever it was, it sure did need ironing!"

GETTING CONFUSED MORE EASILY

I find the old brain just seems to get a little confused at times. Like the little old lady who was stopped by the state patrol:

"Lady, the minimum speed on this highway is 40 miles an hour. We have clocked you at just 20 miles an hour, and you are holding up traffic."

"But the sign right over there says the speed limit is 20 miles an hour," she argued.

"No, ma'am. That's not the speed limit, it's the highway number. You are driving on Route 20. And by the way, why do the other three ladies in your car look so frightened?"

"I don't know," she replied. "Unless it's because we just came off Route 119."

CAN'T DO THINGS I USED TO

As I get older, I am unhappy that my physical abilities just aren't what they used to be. For example, you may have also noticed that steps are steeper than they used to be. What I can't understand is, if medical science has improved so much in the past 50 years, why was I so much healthier and in better shape back then than I am now?

I can sympathize with the 86 year old Irishman, Sean Murphy. He had been fixed up with a blind date with the

Widow O'Rourke. Mrs. O'Rourke's daughter was concerned and curious about how things would transpire, and anxiously awaited her mother's return from the date.

"How did the date go?" she asked her momma when she returned.

"I had to slap his face six times," her mother said indignantly.

"He got that fresh, did he?"

"No, I was trying to keep him awake."

"If it works, it hurts—if it doesn't hurt, it probably ain't working," has become the general rule relative to the parts of my body. Another example of the loss of function that goes along with aging:

A 90 year old couple fell in love, got married, and went on a two week honeymoon.

"How was the honeymoon?" asked one of the bride's friends when she returned.

"We had a good time," she replied.

"You know that's not what I meant. What I want to know is how often you made love," she said with a leer.

"Almost every night."

"Really?!" she said unbelievingly.

"Really. Almost on Monday night, almost on Tuesday night, almost on Wednesday.................."

LAME EXCUSES

The reason I dislike lame excuses is that they're probably not going to work. For example, we're undergoing a bad cold spell, and night before last at 4:00 AM, the furnace began making odd vibration noises.

With my lousy hearing, I wouldn't have heard or known about it, and gone on sleeping blissfully. However, What's

Her Name has extremely acute hearing, and the noise woke her up. (What's Her Name is my bride, whom I cannot identify by name, because she has told me that if I write about her she will pound knots upon my head.)

Like all wives, she loves to share such events with her husband, so shook me awake to tell me the furnace was making noise. I thanked her profusely for awakening me to impart this fascinating bit of information. "What's causing the noise?" she asked me. "How the hell should I know?" was my tender response.

Aldous Huxley once said the secret of life can be summed up in just five words, "You get used to it." My philosophy of life is instead, "If you ignore things, they may go away." Besides I didn't think it too healthy an idea to phone Haskell Perry, the guy who owns the heating company, at 4:00 AM with outside temperatures at 15 degrees, and wake him from a sound sleep to tell him, "My furnace is making a funny noise."

"A pine cone has probably dropped in the fan on the tower outdoors, and is causing the vibration," was the only feeble (and stupid) excuse I could come up with in order to hopefully get WHN to ignore it so I could go back to sleep.

Fortunately the noise stopped, and we were able to get back to sleep.

Until about 30 minutes later when I was again awakened by her, as she said accusingly:

"We don't have any pine trees or pine cones in our yard!"

The best lame excuse I ever heard came from ex-footballer Alex Hawkins. He was known to carouse and imbibe strong spirits quite often. One cold winter's night, in an inebriated condition, he didn't get home until 7:00 AM.

"Where have you been all night?!" remonstrated his wife.

"Well," said Alex, "I got home at 11:30, but I had forgotten my key, and I didn't want to wake you up, so I slept in the hammock in the back yard all night."

"That's interesting," said his wife. "We took the hammock down three weeks ago!"

"Nevertheless," responded Hawkins with great dignity. "That's my story and I'm stickin' with it."

PROFUNDITIES

Another vexation of mine is the habit we all have of meekly accepting things as the truth simply because they have been repeated over and over. But Jim Moran was made of sterner stuff. A Public Relations practitioner back in the 1930's, he made a habit of researching and testing such profundities:

"As destructive as a bull in a china shop."

"People are always taking about a bull in a china shop," said Moran. "They have no scientific basis for the remark. How do they know what a bull would do in a china shop?"

So he got permission from the owners of a fine china shop on 5th Avenue in New York to turn a bull loose in their store. He guaranteed of course to pay for all damages. When he turned him loose, the bull just stood there. After awhile he began walking, but he moved carefully, avoiding tables and counters.

The only breakage occurred when one of the observers backed into a small table, breaking a few pieces of china.

"Don't shoot until you see the whites of their eyes."

To test this hypothesis, Moran began by running the following ad in the Boston papers:

"Wanted---12 men for one day's work. Salary $4. Must have following qualifications: Numbers 1and 2 must be nearsighted, 3 and 4 must be farsighted, 5 and 6 must have normal vision, 7 and 8 must be bleary eyed, 9 and 10 must be bright eyed, 11 must have pinkeye, 12 must be cross-eyed."

With the help of an oculist, the 12 men were selected. The nearsighted, farsighted, and normal-sighted men were dressed in American colonial costumes. The bleary eyed, bright-eyed, pink-eyed and cross-eyed were given British redcoat uniforms.

"Now," Jim addressed his two armies, "we are going to re-enact the Battle of Bunker Hill. I am going to prove that when Colonel Prescott shouted, 'Don't fire until you see the whites of their eyes,' he was uttering the stupidest command ever heard on a battlefield."

He gave his two armies old muskets loaded with blanks, and they took their places. Up the hill came the redcoats. Moran called out Prescott's command.

Rather than all the Americans shooting at the same time, the distances at which they fired varied all the way from 75 feet to three feet.

"I never saw a purple cow, I never hope to see one. But I can tell you anyhow, I'd rather see than be one."

One morning Moran awoke with a hangover and had the misfortune to pick up a poetry anthology. The first line of the above poem insinuated itself into his consciousness, and he couldn't get rid of it. Thus he gradually worked up a fine hate for the poem's author, Gelett Burgess.

A few days later, the phone rang in Burgess's apartment. He was asked to come to the lobby where he found Moran and a cow that had been dyed purple all over. Except for three teats that were dyed gold, and the other one silver.

Burgess swore he would never forget the sight as long as he lived.

THINGS THAT ARE "GOOD FOR YOU"

I find I am suspicious of anything that is presented to me as being "good for me." It's probable that childhood experiences have ingrained this phobia in me. Back then I could always tell something was going to happen that I wasn't going to like, when I heard, "It's good for you."

Comedian Alan King told of a conversation at the dinner table when he was a child:

"Eat your vegetables," said his father.

"Why?" asked Alan.

"Because they're good for you."

"Why are they good for me?"

"Because I'm gonna swat you across the head if you don't eat them---that's why they're good for you!"

This logic was probably as good or better than my parents'. They had not the benefit of today's nutritional and vitamin research, to determine what was good for me. They didn't need it.

They had a very simple method of determining the nutritional value of any food, namely that if it tasted bad and I didn't like it, then it was good for me.

The same principle applied to medicines. The worse it tasted the more miraculous its curative powers. (Remember castor oil?) In addition the more it cost, the better it was for you.

One of the most difficult things in life is trying to shove a spoonful of medicine into the gullet of an unwilling child. That's what my father was attempting one day with my sobbing four year old brother. After three spoonfuls had been deposited on his shirt, my old man began to lose his temper.

"This medicine cost a lot of money, and you're going to take it!" he thundered. Finally he was able hold his son's nose, and when he opened his mouth to breathe, was able to thrust a spoonful down his throat. He began to gag, and tearfully said to our father, "If we can afford it, I think I'm going to throw up." (true story)

Since my childhood occurred during the depression of the 1930's when money was scarce, my parents had a corollary maxim regarding food: If it's cheap and plentiful, it's also good for you.

My father had a vegetable garden every summer. The Jolly Green Giant he was not. Every year we'd get a few woody radishes, a few ears of tough corn, and a whole lot of weeds. His one triumph every year was green beans. The man was a world class expert when it came to green beans. Every year he produced a bumper crop, and I do mean bumper!

For 5-6 weeks every summer we ate them at EVERY meal, until they were coming out our ears. The highlight of my summers was when the last green bean had been consumed.

My parent's other food theory was to feed the most fattening, and therefore tastiest, food to the scrawniest child. In those days, milk was not homogenized, and the cream rose to the top. Our youngest brother was skinny, so he was given the cream off the top, while my other brother and I drank the remaining skim milk.

I'll have to admit, however, that their theory worked. My middle brother weighed about 170 pounds when he passed away, and I weigh in at 180. Baby brother has maintained a weight of 260 for many years.

Also "good for me" was to take ballroom dancing lessons when I was about 12 years old, so that I could attain the social graces for when I later began to date. This I hated with a purple passion. To make matters worse, I was always paired with Louise Weiss, who was almost full grown at age 12, while I was still a little squirt. Thus she was a head taller than I was, outweighed me by about 40 pounds, and was a helluva lot stronger. Thus she could jerk me across the floor in any manner she wished.

Anyway, these childhood experiences are the reason I become suspicious about anything that's "good for me."

BEING A WAR HERO

This really is not a peeve, but rather an embarrassment. The public seems to address all World War II veterans as having been heroes. I wasn't. Being a hero involves doing something courageous that you don't HAVE to do. And I had no choice as to whether I would be a participant.

I was in college when World War II broke out. All males of my age who were in good physical condition (1-A classification) were thus scheduled to be drafted into the army. It wasn't a matter of volunteering. The only way to get around the army draft was to join some other branch of the service.

"I'd rather ride than walk," I figured when deciding which branch in which to enlist. "So that eliminates the Army and the Marines, and leaves the Air Force and the Navy. Further if something happens to a plane, I don't know how to fly. If something happens to a ship, I do know how to swim." That was my cowardly thought process in deciding to enlist in the Navy.

Thus it wasn't by choice that I served in the Iwo Jima and Okinawa campaigns, with their kamikaze attacks. To quote three Navy "heroes" during naval campaigns:

"I have not yet begun to fight," proclaimed Admiral John Paul Jones

"Damn the torpedoes, full speed ahead," said Admiral Farragut

"I wish I was home," whined Ensign Jack Runninger

"What sea duty do you prefer?" I was asked by Naval personnel after I finished training. I figured I would play along with the game, since I knew they weren't going to take my desires into account anyway. So I replied:

"Tug boat duty in San Francisco Bay."

"Aren't you a red blooded American?" he asked.

"Yes," I said. "But that doesn't mean I want to see it spilled."

I hasten to add that there WERE MANY heroes in World War II who did courageous things they didn't have to do. I just didn't happen to be one of them, so it's sort of embarrassing being viewed as such.

CHRISTMAS NEWSLETTERS

Many of these are fine. Particularly from close friends who are letting me know what has happened in their lives the past year.

The ones that irk me come from folks I really don't know that well, and the ones that do nothing but boast about the accomplishments of their offspring, and go into detail about their health problems.

The wife of a deceased distant relative, who I've never met, sends me a Christmas two page single spaced bragging newsletter every year. As best I can tell, none of her children or grandchildren have as yet received a Nobel Prize. However this seems to be about the only honor they haven't achieved.

In addition to the description of all the remarkable things they have accomplished over the past year, she further brightens my holiday season with a detailed history of her surgeries and health problems during the previous year.

In the spirit of Scrooge, I have often been tempted to send her the following newsletter, but never have had the guts to do so:

"We've had a real good year since last Xmas. We're right proud of our granddaughter, Lavonia. She was elected president of the sophomore class! It's the first time in the history of the school that anyone has been elected president of the sophomore class three years in a row.

"Our eldest son, Ezra, received a reward for good behavior. It got him out of prison two years early. And we're right proud of our baby granddaughter, Tessie Lou. She was selected as the poster child for the Zero Population Growth movement.

"Also you may remember our youngest son, Clem, who was an unwanted child. He's really come up in the world. Now he's wanted in 12 states! Our youngest daughter Rachel Lou, has graduated from high school in just three terms. (Clinton's, Bush's, and Obama's.)"

I may also describe my hemorrhoid surgery in detail (no pun intended). That ought to brighten her holiday season as much as she brightens mine.

FEMALE MEMORIES

It doesn't seem fair that females have such amazing, but selective, memories.

Let's assume that you have been married 25 years. Thus you have had 25 anniversaries and 25 birthdays to remember. Let us further assume that you have "done good" and remembered 49 of the 50 with some sort of present. Which do you think your bride is going to remember, the 49 successes or the one miss?

This memory trait has been noted by many men wiser than I.

"Even more important than remembering birthday and anniversaries is remembering what happened the day you were supposed to remember a day, and failed to do so," said George Burns.

"My wife is afflicted with total recall," was S. J. Perelman's observation.

"I lost my car keys one time almost 20 years ago," said Bill Cosby. "Ever since, my wife keeps telling the children, 'your father always loses his car keys.'"

"When my wife discovered what I'd done, she got historical," a friend told me.

"You mean 'hysterical' do you not?" I responded.

"No, I mean 'historical'. She remembered and brought up everything I'd ever done wrong during our entire marriage!"

At least this memory faculty has one advantage. Husband's can be forgiven for forgetting their mistakes. After all, there's no sense in two people remembering the same thing.

FEMALE LOGIC

Female logic is not only difficult to understand, but even more difficult to refute. This trait is either inborn or acquired at an early age.

"Eat your squash or you can't have any dessert!" I thundered at daughter Janet as she toyed with her food when she was about four years old.

"I don't like squish squash," she pouted.

"Why don't you like it?" I asked.

"Because I've never tried it before."

Just how are you going to argue with female logic like that? Another example:

"The car won't start," a woman phoned her husband.

"What's wrong with it?" he asked.

"It has water in the carburetor."

"Where is the car?"

"In the lake."

And wifely logic about who is responsible for what is somewhat confusing:

"I'm hot," Jeff Foxworthy reports his wife told him in the middle of the night, during their second year of marriage. "So I got up to turn on the ceiling fan. On the way back to bed, it dawned on me, 'Whoa. Why am I doing this? I'm not hot.'"

But I heard of another gentleman, with much longer marriage experience and wisdom, who had a similar problem. He was attending a convention at which the headquarters hotel was completely sold out. Therefore at the request of the hotel management, he agreed to let a lady he didn't know share his room.

"I'm cold," he heard the lady in the other bed say seductively, just as he got to sleep. So he got up and closed the window. As he was nodding off again, he heard her again say, again seductively, "I'm still cold. Could you get me a blanket?"

"Would you like to pretend that we're man and wife so that you won't be cold?" he asked her.

"Oh, yes," she replied enthusiastically, looking forward to sharing his bed.

"Then get up and get your own damn blanket!"

DE-PERSONALIZED SERVICE

"This is Sheriff Joe Adams calling," began the phone call I received almost 60 years ago. "You have been accused of passing a worthless check, and I'd appreciate it if you'd turn yourself in."

Fortunately I recognized that the voice was not that of Sheriff Adams, but instead of Sim Dodd, the vice president at the bank I used. He had phoned to let me know that my account was overdrawn, so that I could make a deposit to cover it without incurring any penalties.

In the past few years I have again twice been a few dollars overdrawn at the bank. Neither time did I receive a helpful call from any bank personnel like Sim Dodd. Each time all I got was a notice that my account had been docked 25 bucks because of it.

Business just isn't as personalized as it used to be. I never seem to be dealing with a person anymore, but instead as a number talking with a computer. Or punching numbers to finally get to the person I need to talk to in any transaction. May be efficient, but it sure is cold and turns me off.

Speaking of banks brings up another thing that is really a peeve, how they suck people into credit card debt, which has financially ruined so many folks with their exorbitant interest rates. Businesses no longer seem to have any moral principles as to what is best for their clients. All they think of any more is how to screw clients out of the most money.

POOR SERVICE

"Taste the soup," said the elderly gentleman.
"What's wrong with it?" said the rude and surly waiter.
"Taste the soup," repeated the man.
"What's the problem, old man? Is it too hot, or too salty, or what?" he said impatiently.
"Taste the soup," the customer said again.
"Okay, okay. Where's the spoon?"
"Ah HAH!" said the diner triumphantly.

It seems nowadays that customers have a helluva time finding someone to wait on them. Then when they do, the clerk, waiter, etc. are often rude, and don't want to be bothered. Or feel it's beneath their dignity.

The late columnist Mike Royko told of going to a restaurant for lunch. It took 15 minutes before a harried waitress brought them menus. She returned 10 minutes later to take their order. Another 20 minutes transpired before their food came. Most of the orders were wrong.

"I'm terribly sorry," she apologized when they complained. "We're terribly short-handed today. One waitress and the regular cook are out."

"Where's the manager?" asked Royko.

"He's over there in that booth with all the computer printouts on the table." Royko walked over to him.

"Nice place you have here," he lied to the manager, and then engaged him in conversation about the restaurant. The manager boasted of how he had established better business principles since taking over. He pointed out the data the computer had provided showing how he had made the restaurant more efficient. He obviously felt this to be more important and more in line with his job description, than pitching in to help.

Royko maintained the restaurant would have better success if it was run by a short Greek who didn't know beans about business principles.

"He would make sure waitresses and cooks showed up, and would pitch in to help cook and wait tables when needed. Which would do a lot better job of retaining customers than studying expense ratios."

Sometimes, too, the waiters just ain't that sharp. "What is the Soup du Jour?" a diner asked his waiter.

"I'll have to check and see," replied the waiter. When he returned to the table he said:

"It's the 'soup of the day.'"

IMPOLITE FOLKS

The flashy looking tourist in a fancy car came to a fork in the road. Not knowing which way to go, he hollered rudely to a farmer working in the field adjacent to the road:

"Hey, Rube! Does it matter which road I take to get to Chattanooga?"

"Not to me, it don't," replied the farmer.

It's always good to see impolite folks get their comeuppance.

However, at times impoliteness may be inadvertent, and embarrass the persons involved. I heard of a woman who went to her doctor, and complained:

"My husband seems to have lost all interest in sex. Is there anything that I can do about it to make him regain it?"

"Yes," replied the doctor. "There is a new drug that seems to work fine in such situations. All you need to do is to slip this pill in his coffee at dinner tonight, and I think you'll find that his passions are slowly aroused. By bedtime he should be ready."

"I think maybe you gave me too strong a pill," the lady told the doctor the next day. "I did as you said, and slipped the pill into his coffee at dinner. He took two quick sips, jumped to his feet, pulled the tablecloth off the table breaking all the dishes, tore off all his and my clothes, threw me down on the table, and made love to me then and there."

"I am so sorry," said the doctor. "Obviously I did give you too strong a dose, and I apologize. To help make up for it, I'd be happy to pay for replacing all the dishes he broke."

"That's not necessary," she replied. "We don't plan to eat at the same restaurant anytime soon anyway."

THOSE WHO ARE ALWAYS RIGHT

"You always seem to maintain that you are right about everything," a man was accused. "Have you ever been wrong?"

"Just once," he replied. "One time I thought I was wrong, but it turned out that I wasn't."

We've all been irritated at times by such people who never admit they are wrong. Wives are often accused of being such know-it-alls.

"I married Miss Right," said a young husband. "What I didn't realize was that her first name was 'Always'."

"For sale: Set of encyclopedias. No longer needed. Wife knows everything," read a classified ad in a newspaper.

Fortunately I do not have that problem at my house. My wife just the other day after a slight disagreement, admitted to me, "You're always right." I was appreciative and thanked her. Until she added, "Some of the time."

SELF-IMPORTANCE

There are some folks I like to term as "Hubcaps." They're the ones who think they are "Big Wheels," but are really much less. Like the guy who was overly impressed with himself, and boasted that he was a self-made man.

"Shows what you get with unskilled labor," whispered an onlooker.

Wives are noticeably expert at keeping their husbands from their self opinions of greatness. Like the guy who stepped on one of those scales that spit out a card with your weight and your fortune.

"The card says I am a leader of men, and irresistible to women," he bragged to his wife.

"It has your weight wrong too," said his wife as she glanced at the card.

SWIFTIES

The late Bub Wilcox and Mike McDougald are the culprits here. I had not heard of Tom Swifties, until they turned me on to this maddening and addictive low form of pun, in which the adverb plays on the rest of the sentence. Here are a few examples, with explanations so you'll know what to look for:

"The prisoner is climbing down the wall," said Tom condescendingly. (The prisoner climbing down the wall is a "con" descending.)

"I can't believe I ate the whole pineapple," said Tom dolefully. (Dole being the brand of pineapple that made him full.)

"The doctor had to remove my left auricle and ventricle," said Tom half-heartedly. (After this surgery, he would be left with only half of his heart.)

This type of pun takes its name from Tom Swift, a fictional boy's adventure hero created by Edward L. Stratemeyer. Under the pseudonym Victor Appleton, he published a series of books featuring the young Tom Swift. Tom was heroic, courageous, pure in nature, and was always the good guy who fought against evil.

His problem was that he always spoke in a strange fashion, and rarely passed a remark without a stilted qualifying and unnecessary adverb, such as "Tom added, *eagerly.*" The punning Swifties arose as a pastiche (ridicule or imitation) of this stilted conversation. Other examples I enjoy include:

"I love hot dogs," said Tom with relish.

"Elvis is dead," said Tom expressly.

"That statue of Venus is my favorite," said Tom disarmingly.

"There's no need for silence," Tom allowed.

"Don't let me drown in Egypt," pleaded Tom, deep in denial.

Even more frustrating is how I find myself wasting time by searching my brain for more examples. I came up with a few, such as, "My birthday is tomorrow," said eight year old Tom benignly (be-nine-ly.)

Not a very productive use of time, and thus again, quite maddening.

CHRISTMAS TOY ASSEMBLY

"There are three stages of life," according to some philosopher whose name escapes me at the moment.

1. When you believe in Santa Claus.
2. When you no longer believe in Santa Claus.
3. When you ARE Santa Claus.

To these I would add a fourth stage. In this stage you are still the Santa banker. But your kids have grown and left the nest so you no longer have to assemble the doohickeys with indecipherable instructions, that Santa and his elves were too lazy to put together. This is one of the few benefits of old age, so becomes much less of a vexation now than when I was younger.

Christmas is supposed to be a religious holiday. But I well remember the many Christmas Eves I almost lost my religion as I attempted to assemble various gadgets.

First of all, I am not exactly noted as an expert handyman. When it comes to putting something together, I have zero fingers and ten thumbs.

Secondly, most of these gizmos seem to be made in Asian countries. So, of course, the original assembly instructions are in an Asian language, and have to be translated into English for the American market. These translators seem to know very little about English grammar. The resultant directions confuse even a graduate engineer, let alone a jackleg like me.

"I have to go home and assemble a Corner Grocery Store," I told a friend one Christmas Eve.

"I put that one together last year," he told me. "Took me four hours!"

And he was a contractor!

I didn't relish the idea of spending the balance of the night working on the contraption. But then dawned a rare bright idea. I printed on the box, "My elves and I didn't have time to put this together for you. Please ask your daddy to do it. Signed Santa Claus."

It took me all day Christmas to put the cotton-pickin' thing together, but at least I got a good night's sleep. And my daughter was very much impressed with getting a personal note from Santa.

On another Christmas Eve, I spent two hours assembling a doll house. Mother-in-law then tripped and fell backwards, coming to rest sitting atop the doll house. Mother-in-law had a rather large "sitter", and it took me another two hours to repair the damage.

I have discovered there is a fifth Santa stage when you get as old as I am. In this stage you become more cantankerous, and become Scrooge rather than Santa.

CENSORSHIP

To illustrate the importance of being observant, I once included the following story in a column I wrote for a national optometric journal:

"I'll bet I can tell where you went to college," said one cocktail party participant to another. "I doubt it," the other gentleman replied. "You're only known me since we met five minutes ago at this party."

"Nevertheless, I think you're a Harvard graduate."

"Your obvious culture and good breeding, impeccable tailoring, excellent vocabulary, gentlemanly manner, and New England accent all led me to this conclusion."

"If you're so durned smart," said another man in the conversational group, "where did I go to college?"

"You went to the U. of Alabama."

"That's right! How could you tell?"

"I saw your school ring when you were picking your nose."

A large contact lens firm published a book of some of the columns I have written for optometric journals over the years. I submitted 150 such columns. The company's legal and marketing departments informed me that 31, including the Alabama story, were politically incorrect and needed to be deleted, to eliminate any risk of their being sued.

Much of the world has evidently lost its ability to laugh itself. We take ourselves too seriously, and look for insults in every situation, rather than humor. Other groups the publisher felt might be offended included:

PREACHERS. The story I told concerns the country preacher whose bicycle was stolen. After much thought he came up with a way to discover the thief.

"I'll preach the Ten Commandments next Sunday," he said to himself. "When I come to 'thou shalt not steal', I'll bear down hard, and the thief may have a guilty conscience and return my bike."

But when he got to "thou shalt not commit adultery," he remembered where he had left his bicycle.

WIVES. Also not acceptable were jests I made about comments husbands should avoid at all costs:

"My wife is a good old gal, comfortable as an old shoe. But like an old shoe, every part of her is worn out except for the tongue."

"The doctor when he examined her, told me, "I don't like the looks of your wife. I told him I didn't either, but she was good to the kids."

"My wife's cooking is so bad, the flies got together and mended the screen door."

To anyone who has felt insulted by any of these, I hasten to say that I'm truly sorry. Not for what I've said, but that there are folks who are so sensitive and insecure that they can't lighten up sufficiently to accept a little harmless ribbing.

BEING A LOUSY FOOTBALL PLAYER

Perhaps my favorite "Peanuts" comic strip was the one in which Linus was excitedly telling Charlie Brown, "You should have been at the football game! Our team was behind by 13 points, with only a minute left to play. We scored two touchdowns in the final minute to win the game. All the fans went wild."

"I wonder how the other team felt," was Charlie's plaintive reaction.

My school days football career made it easy to empathize with Charlie. It is very vexing to have an extreme love for sports, and be as lousy an athlete as I was. I was never large, nor strong, nor coordinated, nor fast.

When I went out for football my freshman year, the coach decided I should be a quarterback, because I made good grades, and thus he felt smart enough to call the proper plays. (Coaches didn't call the plays back in those days.) I soon showed this "intelligence" in the first game against Joliet. I was the deep man on the kickoff, and let the ball roll dead in the end zone for what I thought was an automatic touchback. Instead one of their players downed the ball for a touchdown. We lost 6-0.

However one time I did show some intelligence when our lightweight (under 140 pounds) team was scrimmaging against the freshman-sophomore heavyweight team. We had fourth down and two at the 50 yard line. The opposition expected us to punt, but I crossed them up by calling for a running play. Which of course failed to pick up the two yards.

"That sure was a stupid play call!" stormed the coach as he pulled me out of the game.

It wasn't near as stupid as he thought. On punts my assignment was to block the opposing left tackle, who would have a full head of steam by the time he got to me in the backfield. The left tackle was Adolph Baum, who weighed 225 against my 115. I was still hurting from the last time we punted, so in play calling opted for self preservation rather than football tactics.

The first team quarterback got injured so I started the game against LaSalle-Peru. LaSalle and Peru were towns in the coal mining area of central Illinois, and had some mighty tough guys.

"LaSalle has the toughest guys in the state, and the farther south you go in town, the tougher they get," a LaSalle resident once told me. "And I live in the LAST house---in the basement!"

Anyway, in those days, there were no offensive and defensive teams, you played both ways. Thus being quarterback on offense automatically made you a defensive back on defense. We lost the game 18-0. All three touchdowns came from their quarterback, name of Gapinski, to the receiver I was supposed to be covering. That was my last starting assignment.

Loving football like I did, made the whole experience quite exasperating.

LOUSY AT BASKETBALL TOO

To set the scene: The C.M. Bardwell grade school lightweight basketball team was playing against Centre Grade School in the finals of the lightweight grade-school tournament. This was back in the 1930's when there was a center jump after every point scored, rather than the opposing team taking the ball out of bounds.

I was the 10-year old standing guard on the Bardwell team. The standing guard was the "defensive specialist." On offense he helped bring the ball up the floor, but was never supposed to penetrate beyond the free throw circle. After noting my speed and agility, Coach Peterson evidently decided I was perfectly suited to be his "standing" guard.

Anyway we had progressed through the first two rounds of the tournament to meet heavily favored Centre in the finals. Centre's shooting was a little off that night, and ours never had been too good, so in the middle of the third quarter the score was tied 3-3.

I dribbled up the floor to my stationary spot back of the free-throw circle and looked for someone to whom I could pass the ball. All my teammates were well covered so finally, in desperation, I took a shot at the basket with a terrific underhand heave. Lo and behold, the ball hit the rim, bounced up, and came down through the hoop, giving us a 5-3 lead.

This so inflated my confidence that I took three or four more shots from the same spot during the next few minutes. None of them came within six feet of the backboard, let alone the basket. Coach Peterson called a time out and informed me that lightning seldom strikes twice in the same place, and to knock it off.

But we held on for a 6-5 victory and the championship. Since I had somehow made a free throw earlier in the game, I was the game's high scorer with 3 points. The next day in school, the whole class applauded when I walked in. As befits any hero, I blushed modestly. Then and there I decided this would be my goal in life, to become an athletic hero with all the adulation that would ensue.

Unfortunately, I peaked too early. As it turned out, this was the highlight of my athletic career. It was nothing but downhill the rest of the way. Never again to did I ever achieve stardom.

MONDEGREENS

A Mondegreen is defined as "a mishearing of a popular phrase or song lyric." The term was coined by writer Sylvia Wright.

As a child she had heard the Scottish ballad, "The Bonny Earl of Murray," and had believed that one stanza went like this:

Ye Highlands and Ye Lowlands
Oh where hae you been?
They hae slay the Earl of Murray,
And Lady Mondegreen.

"Poor Lady Mondegreen," thought Sylvia Wright. "A tragic heroine dying with her liege—how poetic." Some years later she discovered that the last two lines of the stanza instead were:

"They hae slay the Earl of Murray,
And laid him on the green." (Rather than "And Lady Mondegreen")

Sylvia was so distraught by the sudden disappearance of her heroine, that she memorialized her with a neologism.

Like puns and Swifties, Mondegreens are addictive and maddening, which is why I list them as a peeve.

Another example of a Mondegreen is the child in Sunday School who drew a picture of a chubby child. When asked the name of the child in the picture, he replied, "Round John Virgin," a figure also found in "Silent Night."

The majority of Mondegreens come from song lyrics. Some examples:

1. "Gladly, the cross-eyed bear," known in the real world as that old hymn, "Gladly the Cross I'd bear."

2. You may remember that touching moment in "I'm In The Mood For Love," when the singer reveals his favorite nickname for his beloved.

"I'm in the mood for love,
Simply because you're near me,
Funny butt, when you're near me......."

According to one expert who collects Mondegreens, the Pledge of Allegiance is such a hotbed of Mondegreens for children, that one could create a composite of submitted entries:

"I pledge a lesion to the flag, of the United States of American, and to the republic for Richard Stans, one naked individual, with liver tea and just this for all."

Mondegreens even extend to book titles. "A Monk Swimming" is the title of a book by Malachy McCourt. When he was a lad growing up in Ireland in the Cahtolic Church, when reciting "Hail Mary, full of grace. The Lord is with Thee. Blessed are thou amongst women," McCourt always heard "amongst women" as instead "A monk swimming."

Another of his books is titled "Harold Be Thy Name," the phrase from the Lord's Prayer which had early established for him God's first name.

However there is another childhood clic that strongly disagrees with him. They maintain that rather than Harold, the Lord's first name is Andy. They cite as their reference the old hymn, "Andy walked with me, Andy talked with me, Andy told me I was his own."

STANDING IN LINE

You have completed your grocery shopping, and are trying to decide which of the three open long checkout lines you should select. (Only three are open even though the store has a total of ten counters. Why they built that many I don't know. I've never seen more than four open at the same time.) You do realize that no matter which line you choose, it's going to be wrong one anyway. Sure enough, the person ahead of you in the line you pick has some sort of problem, after you've already had a long wait for slow customers ahead of you.

This requires their tracking down two assistant managers, and finally the manager to come to the counter to sort out the matter. All of which takes seemingly forever. During this time you watch shoppers breeze quickly through the lines you did not choose. Some of these shoppers had not even entered the store to begin shopping while you were already standing in the molasses line. Some probably hadn't even left home.

Finally the problem in your line has been resolved, and the lady is told her correct charge. Only then does she pull out of her purse tons of coupons, so the whole thing has to be refigured. At which point she begins to search in the convoluted snarl of multitudinous items in a purse as large as a suitcase for her checkbook. After a ten minute search she finds it, and then laboriously begins to record the amount on her Transaction Register, subtract it to get her new balance, and only then fill out the spaces on her check, the date, the amount, the store name, and her signature. Most of which she could and should have filled in beforehand, or after she returns home.

Understanding this peeve, I could readily appreciate how the growing line behind us in the store was becoming restless and even hostile. My wife and I were the culprits rather than the recipients. She had brought her work credit card, rather than her personal one, so one of those long conferences with managers ensued, keeping the line from moving.

"May I go home with you?" I asked the man in line behind me who had only a large flat screen TV, and a case of beer in his cart, in an attempt to make light of the hold up. However, he didn't seem to think the remark particularly funny, and continued scowling about the hold up.

Finally they got the matter straightened out, and I was relieved about being able to depart and no longer suffer the scornful stares behind me. But then we discovered that a chicken we had purchased was billed to us at $9,941.61. We felt that was a little expensive for chicken, so there was a further wait while this was corrected.

Post office lines are another irritant. It always seems that there is an inverse ratio between the length of the line and the number of employees manning the windows. And there is always someone ahead of you who asks the clerk 438 questions, or is lonesome and thus wants to engage the clerk in conversational pleasantries about the weather, etc., while the rest of the line fumes.

THE GPS LADY

I have a lousy sense of direction. I have lived in Rome, GA for more than 60 years, and still have difficulty remembering the route I need to take to various locations. Thus my new bride purchased for me as a Christmas present, a GPS navigation system. If nothing else, it looks extremely impressive on my dash board!

For those of you ignorant about GPS's as I was, it is some sort of satellite system whereby you punch in your home address and your destination address, and some lady who is apparently sitting in the satellite tells you each turn you should make to get there. This lady can be very pleasant as long as you follow her commands.

But if you make or miss a turn with which she disagrees, she goes crazy and is the rudest, most annoying, person I've ever known! Every few minutes she sarcastically says in a "you sure are a dumb ass" tone of voice, "RE-CAL-CU-

LATING!" And then impatiently tries to get you to make turns to get you to return to that spot, rather than continuing toward your destination.

In addition when I enter my home address as the starting point of the trip, the GPS informs me there is no such place. Perhaps I'm hallucinating about living there? So I have to go to a different neighborhood, and enter some stranger's address in order to get the lady to condescend to give me directions to my destination.

But perhaps I am being unfair to this lady. I've heard her voice on other folks' GPS's, and was surprised to learn that she was not giving me her exclusive attention. There has to be millions of GPS' in operation, and I don't see how she finds time to supervise my trip along with all the others.

So I shouldn't take her rudeness personally. Obviously with that many trips she is directing, she really doesn't give a damn whether I get there or not.

But why purchase this device, and have to listen to her exasperated tone of voice? When I screw up going somewhere, I can get that same tone of voice from my wife for free.

COMPUTERS

My problem with computers is that I hate it when inanimate objects are smarter than I am. And they get smarter all the time, while I don't. I heard recently of a new unbelievable program.

"This computer program is so advanced, it can answer any question about any person, merely by entering the person's name and social security number," a computer engineer told my friend.

"I don't believe it! That's impossible!" replied my friend.

"I'll demonstrate it to you. Just enter your name, social security number, and the question you want to ask."

"Where is my father?" was the question he entered, along with his SS number. A few minutes later, the answer appeared on the screen---"Your father is fishing in northern Kentucky."

"See, I told you that you were wrong," said my friend. "My father has been dead for ten years."

"First time I've seen it wrong," said the engineer. "However this program is semantically oriented. Perhaps if you rephrase the question."

"Okay. Change the question to, 'Where is my mother's husband?'"

"Your mother's husband has been dead for ten years," read the new reply. "But your father is still fishing in northern Kentucky."

IRISH BULLS

Paddy O'Rourke always slept with a pistol under his pillow in case of a burglarly. One night he thought he heard an intruder enter his room, so fired his pistol toward the bedroom entrance at the foot of the bed. And shot his big toe off.

"It's a good thing I wasn't sleepin' at the other end of the bed," he said to himself. "Or else I'd have shot me brains out."

This is an example of an Irish Bull, defined as statements that are made ludicrous by their incongruous logic. Like Mondegreens and Swifties, I must admit I do enjoy them. My only excuse for listing them as a peeve, is that they also are maddening and addictive.

"Dogs must be carried on the escalator," read a sign by the escalator of an Irish department store. "Where in the world am I going to find a dog at this hour of the day?" said McNamara as he read the sign before boarding the escalator. Another Irish Bull:

"I was one of 15 kids," said Mickey O'Brien. "All us kids kept our mother on a pedestal. We had to, in order to keep her away from me father."

Irish Bulls are not confined to the Irish. The dialogue from Norm in a "Cheers" TV show is another example of such incongruous logic:

"A herd of buffalo can only move as fast as its slowest member. And when the herd is hunted, it is the slowest and weakest ones at the back that are killed first. This natural selection is good for the herd as a whole, because the general speed and health of the whole group keeps improving with the regular killing of the weakest members.

"In much the same way, the human brain can only operate as fast as the slowest brain cells. Now, as we know, excessive intake of alcohol kills brain cells. But naturally it attacks the slowest and weakest brain cells first. In this way, regular consumption of beer eliminates the weaker brain cells, making the brain a faster and more efficient machine.

"That's why you always feel smarter after a few beers."

CAJUN STORIES

Cajun stories are another subject with which I have a love/hate relationship. Like puns, they are groaners, but at the same time I can't help but enjoy them. Three examples follow:

1. Boudreaux and Pierre was walkin' through the woods one day, when he says, "Whooee, Pierre, look at dat big hole! I wonder how deep it goes." They find a rock, and trow

it into da hole, listenin' to see how long it will take to hit the bottom. They don't hear nothin', so look for something bigger to trow in.

Boudreaux notices a railroad tie lyin' in the bushes, picks it up, and trows it in the hole. While they are listenin' for it to hit bottom, a little billy goat comes runnin' out of the bushes, and jumped right into dat deep hole.

A few minutes later their friend Thibodaux comes walkin' out of the bushes, and asks, "Has anyone seen my little billy goat?"

"You wanna hear somethin' strange?" said Boudreaux. "A little billy goat just a couple of minutes ago, came runnin' out of them bushes, and jumped right in that hole right dere."

"Couldn't have been my billy goat," said Thibodeaux. "My little billy goat was tied to a railroad tie back in dose bushes."

2. Boudreaux's first military assignment was advisin' new recruits about their GI insurance. Before long, the captain began noticin' that he was getting a 99 percent signup for the most expensive policy. This was odd, becaue it would cost these poor inductees nearly $30 a month extra. So he decides to sit in on the next session to observe.

Boudreaux's sales pitch.

"If you have da normal GI insurance and go to Iraq and get killed,"said

Boudreaux to the recruits, "da government pays your family $6,000. If you take out the more expensive insurance, which cost you only $30 a month, the government has to pay dem $200,000.

"Now," he concluded, "which bunch you tink they gonna send to Iraq first?"

3. Boudreaux been fishin' down da bayou all day, when he seen a big snake wif a frog in his mouf. He knowed big

bass like dem frogs, so he decided he is gonna steal it from the snake. Dat snake be a cotton mouf water moccasin, so he had to be real careful how he handles him.

He snuk up behin' dat snake and grabbed him round da head. Now Boudreaux know dat he cain't let go of dat snake or he's gonna bite him. But he had a plan. He takes a pint of moonshine likker out of his bib overalls, and pours some in da snake's mouf. The snake kinder rolls his eyeballs, and lets loose of the frog. And Boudreaux toss dat snake back in the bayou.

He goes back to fishin', and a while later he feels somepin' tappin' on his barefoot toes. He look down, and dere wuz dat same snake---wit' two more frogs.

PUNS

Puns are not so much a pet peeve, as they are a vexation. They make me groan, as I suspect they do you as well. As Jane Gray Collier emailed me after I sent her the puns below, "Arghhhhh!!" I thought I had heard them all, but recently Sam Specter sent me a few I hadn't heard. Since I don't want to suffer alone, here they are:

- King Ozymandias of Assyria was running low on cash. His last great possession was the Star of the Euphrates, the most valuable diamond in the ancient world. Desperate, he went to Croesus, the pawnbroker to ask for a loan.

"I'll give you 100,000 dinars for it," said Croesus.

"But I paid a million dinars for it," the king protested. "Don't you know who I am? I am the king!"

"When you wish to pawn a Star, makes no difference who you are," replied Croesus.

- Evidence has been found that William Tell and his family were avid bowlers. Unfortunately, the Swiss league records were destroyed in a fire....so we'll never know for whom the Tells bowled.

- An Indian chief was was sick, so summoned the medicine man. After an exam, the medicine man gave the chief a long, thin strip of elk rawhide, and told him to bite off, chew, and swallow one inch of the leather every day. After a month the medicine man returned to see how the chief was feeling. Said the chief:

"The thong is ended, but the malady lingers on."

It would probably not be wise to inflict further such on you. As friend Wilson Adams said when I sent these to him, "I sure am happy there weren't but three of them!"

SENIOR TENNIS

I have played tennis all my life. Thus I am exasperated by how different the game is, now that I and my tennis buddies have gotten old. Not only is there a decay in athletic skills, but also deterioration in other involved areas, such as memory, hearing, and bladder control.

A typical match can go something like the following. Although all of the incidents I relate did not happen in the same match, every one of them occurred at one time or another.

10:00 AM---Players arrive at courts. One participant has come well prepared. He has neck brace, hat, sunglasses, can of balls, sun lotion, towel, and sweat band. Has forgotten only one thing---his tennis racket.

10:15 AM---Match finally begins after he finds racket to borrow.

10:22 AM---Match is halted while one of the players removes his shoe to adjust his ankle brace.

10:28 AM---Long discussion ensues because no one can remember after the interruption what the score is.

10:34 AM---Finally reach tentative agreement on the game score, but now can't remember whose serve it is.

10:40 AM---Match is halted while one participant rubs Bengay on his shoulder. Has addition beneficial effect, since everyone else's sinus's are now cleared by the penetrating odor "eau de Bengay." Match resumes as soon as everyone's eyes quit watering from the fumes.

10:55 AM---Match again halted as one prostate afflicted player heeds the call of nature, and heads for the restroom.

11:00 AM---Player returns, but now cannot find his racket. Search ensues. Problem finally solved when it is discovered that I have his racket.

11:01 AM---Now we have to search for my racket.

11:04 AM---Too much time has elapsed, necessitating another argument about the score. And whose serve it is.

11:08 AM---Another player finds that he must interrupt the match to go to the bathroom.

11:12 AM---He returns, and third and fourth players decide they had better go too.

11:17 AM---Discussion again as to score, who is serving, ad infinitum.

Memory deterioration is not the only problem in score keeping by us over-the-hill players. The loss of hearing ability also presents problems.

"What's the score?" calls out one of the players to an opponent across the net.

"What?" he responds.

"I said 'What's the score?'" he this time shouts loudly.

"I think it's 30-15."

"I don't think that's right. I think it's 30-15."

However the hearing problem may be a blessing. At times it keeps one from hearing the snide remarks from other players grown crotchety in their old age. Such as:

"You must have forgotten to take your medication this morning," says Herb Blumberg to Charlie Rutledge when he forgets whose serve it is.

"I played poorly last set because I was overconfident," Jerry Hubbard tells me. "But I certainly won't have that problem now that you're my partner."

"There's nothing worse than having a smartass for a partner," I reply.

"Yeah, there is," he one-ups me. "Having a dumbass like you for a partner."

11:40 AM—The match is finally over, and the players wend their way homeward.

However, two of them soon return to pick up the tennis racket and jacket they forgot.

BEING A LOUSY GOLFER

They met at a party, fell in love, and got married the next day.

"I should have told you before we got married," confessed the groom, "that golf is my obsession. I play nine holes every day after work, and 36 holes on Saturday and Sunday, so I won't be home very much."

"There's something I should have told you, too," she sobbed. "I'm a hooker."

"That's no problem," he said. "All we have to do is adjust your grip, and I'll have you hitting the ball straight in no time."

Lots of golfers have this kind of obsession with golf. I possibly would also---if it wasn't for the fact that I have always been such a lousy golfer. The way I play, golf should be spelled backwards---flog. Thus golf has become a peeve for me rather than a joy.

Another example of an obsessed golfer: He was preparing to putt, when a funeral procession passed by on the road next to the golf course. He removed his hat and held it over his heart until the procession had gone by.

"That was certainly a class thing to do," his golfing partner told him.

"It was the least I could do," he replied. "We would have been married 40 years tomorrow."

Friendship flies out the window when golfers compete, even when only small sums are wagered. My friend Clayton Doss and his opponents were once tied going into the last hole. One of his opponents, who was a close friend, hit his second shot straight at the green, but it was not apparent whether it cleared the trap in front.

"Is my good friend in the trap?" asked Doss. "Or is the sumbitch on the green?"

I did hear of one golfer who apparently cured his addiction to the game one day when he was playing horribly. When he got to the last hole, he angrily threw his clubs into the lake, and stalked off. A few minutes later, his partners were relieved to see him contritely return, and wade into the lake to retrieve the clubs.

When he got back ashore, he opened a pocket on the golf bag, took out his car keys, and threw the bag and clubs back into the lake.

LEGAL ODDITIES

Hal Lucination is an alien from outer space, who came to visit me four or five years ago.

"I'm sure there are probably reasons for some of the actions of you Earthlings," he told me. "But I swear some of them seem awfully strange to an outsider like me.

"For example, the prisoner who broke loose from a deputy, and killed a judge and other court workers in Atlanta. Now his attorneys say that the case should be tried away from Atlanta, because there are too many people there who saw him do it! I thought the purpose of your trials was to determine if the accused did indeed do the act, so wouldn't it make sense to have the trial take place where it was observed?"

"And then I read that just prior to the execution of a prisoner, it was necessary to have him undergo a physical examination by a doctor. What happens if he fails the exam? Is he then released since he is not sufficiently well to undergo the execution?"

"Does seem a bit odd," I conceded. "Any other such observations?"

"I also saw a news story about ten city of Atlanta employees who embezzled money from the city by making false claims. The harsh punishment they received was………..paid vacations?!!!!!"

"It was a suspension with pay," I remonstrated.

"Maybe so. But that's still a paid vacation."

"And a nine year old girl is abducted by a known sex offender, who admits to then raping and killing her. A news story says that after he was arrested, this monster was put under suicide watch in his jail cell. Why would they want to stop him?!

"Then there's the case of the 15 year old girl who stabbed to death her grandparents. Her attorney complained that the poor girl was upset when no one testified in her behalf at the court hearing. That's sort of like the story about the lad who murdered his parents, and then expected pity and mercy from the court because he was an orphan.

"And I read a headline in one of your newspapers that said, 'Severed Head Discovered in Lake. Police Suspect

Foul Play'. Do they think that possibly the man's hand slipped while he was shaving?

"Also I saw where some idiot purchased a toasted cheese sandwich on Ebay for $30,000, because it purportedly had the image of the Virgin Mary on it.

"These are just some of the reasons it appears to me you have a rather weird world here," Mr. Lucination told me prior to returning to his native planet.

Come to think of it, it may also seem rather weird that I would expect anyone to believe that I had spoken with someone from another planet.

SNAKES

"You can always tell a poisonous snake from a non-poisonous snake," our guide in the Okefenokee Swamp told us. "The pupils of the eyes are a slit on poisonous snakes, and round on non-poisonous ones."

That is without doubt the most useless advice I have ever received. When encountering a snake, I have no intention of moving close enough to perform an eye examination. And if I should happen to be close enough to see its eyes when first spotting said snake, my brain will be occupied with giving signals to my feet to move rapidly away, rather than doing a snake eye examination.

However I did hear about an optometrist who did do an eye examination on a snake. He found him to be extremely nearsighted. He couldn't fit him with glasses because the snake of course had no ears on which to hang them. So instead he prescribed and fitted contact lenses.

"You have not only corrected my vision difficulty," enthused the snake to the optometrist a few days later, "you've also solved my love life problem."

"How could that be?"

"When I got to where I could see, I discovered I'd been shacking up with a garden hose."

Recently I read about a couple who had a bad snake experience, which occurred while they were flying from Houston to New York. It seems the idiot in the seat in front of them was carrying a large python in his gym bag, which he placed beneath his seat. The python got loose, and slithered in the couple's direction.

Can you picture watching a very large snake emerging from a bag next to your feet, and slithering up toward you? While you are locked in your seat by a seat belt? If it had been me, my chief concern would have been whether my carry on bag contained a clean pair of under shorts.

To be fair, I did hear of another case in which snakes performed a helpful service. Two country boys were going on a camping trip. Each had a bag slung over his shoulder.

"What's in the bag?" someone asked the first man.

"I got me a couple of quarts of moonshine whiskey in case of snake bite."

"What's in your bag?" he asked the second.

"A couple of snakes."

"If it ain't got no shoulders, fergit it!" Lewis Grizzard used to quote a boyhood chum. My sentiments exactly.

WOMEN WHO THINK MEN INSENSITIVE

"Au contraire," is my response to the assumption expressed by many women that their husbands are insensitive. For example humorist Robert Steed once told about J.D. "Goat" Rankin, a "paradigm of husbandly sensitivity."

"His sensitivity manifested itself in many ways," wrote Steed. "First and foremost, though he eschewed regular hours and gainful employment for himself, he was always sufficiently thoughtful to see that his wife had a good job."

Another example he cited was in reference to a bus picking him up at his home, for a trip to the state basketball tournament. As he boarded the bus his wife said plaintively, "J.D., we don't have any stovewood cut."

"Don't worry, honey," Goat replied in a tone so soft and suave that it could have been issued by Ronald Coleman, "I ain't takin' the axe."

Modern man has let things get out of control. On a trip I took to Africa a few years ago, I noted two native women busily building a hut in a rural area, while five men sat under a tree playing some game. The reason was explained to us that in olden days, men there were the hunters and warriors, while women stayed home and did all the work. Since hunting and fighting were no longer necessary, the men had decided that this division of responsibility was still a good idea.

And they call them primitive and less intelligent?!

I must admit that women are superior in some respects. For example, Fred Astaire received accolades for being such a marvelous dancer. Yet his partner, Ginger Rogers, did the same steps---- and did them on high heels----and moving backward.

And most wives are extremely helpful to their husbands. I recently heard about a wife who was perhaps a bit too helpful:

"Have you ever been unfaithful to me?" asked her husband.

"Yes," she admitted, " but only for your benefit.

"How can your unfaithfulness be beneficial to me?" he asked.

"Well, do you remember when the bank was preparing to foreclose on our house mortgage? I slept with the bank president in order to get him not to do so. And do you remember when your boss was going to fire you, but then didn't? It's because I agreed to sleep with him also."

"In that case I guess I can forgive you. But were there any other instances?"

"Well, yes," she replied. "Do you remember when you had your heart set on being elected president of your lodge, and you were 14 votes short?"

It appears to me that too much sensitivity can at times be worse than being a little insensitive. At a meeting in Atlanta, a Tennessee lady boasted to me that her husband never went to any out of town meetings without asking her to go along.

"I know," I replied unwisely. "He told me he'd rather take you with him, than have to kiss you goodbye."

I thought it was kind of funny. She didn't!

PRACTICAL JOKES

Unfortunately I must confess that practical jokes are a pet peeve only when they are played on me. When done to others, I then seem to find them funny. The two best (or worst) I've ever heard were both reported by the late Mike Royko:

Four friends were on a fishing trip. It was 10:00 PM. They had fished all day, had a few beers, played some poker, and were going to turn in and get up before dawn for more fishing. One, named Joe, was the first to his bunk. He was exhausted. Within a few moments he was snoring.

Suddenly a brilliant idea came to one of his "friends" which he quickly explained to the others. One of them got Joe's wristwatch, and changed the time to 4:45 AM. Then they changed their own watches and the time on the alarm clock to read the same.

They set the alarm to go off at 5:00 AM, turned off all the lights, took off their clothes, and went to bed. Fifteen minutes later, the alarm clock went off. They all got up, shuffling around, making the grumbly, miserable sounds that men make early in the morning. One of them fixed toast and coffee.

The most miserable was Joe. He sat on the edge of the bed, shaking his head and moaning, "I don't feel like I've been to bed at all. I must be getting old" he said as they dropped anchor and began fishing at what he thought to be 5:45 AM (but actually at 11:00 PM the night before.)

"Boy it's dark," he kept saying. Finally when his watch said almost 7:00 AM, he asked, "Shouldn't it be getting light by now?"

"Daylight savings," one of his companions replied.

When another hour passed without any sign of the sky lightening in the east, he finally caught on to what had happened. Reportedly they had to wrestle an oar out of his hands.

The other Royko story concerns the Chicago salesman who became bored at the ritual of sending out Christmas cards. So he got an idea.

"You know how folks will write a few personal lines on a card? Well, here's what I did. If a guy had been in the service, I'd write on the card I sent him something like, 'Hi, Joe, old buddy. Got your address from Jim Scanlon (you remember the old barracks moocher.) Me and the wife and kids are going to be passing through Chicago during the Christmas holidays, so we'll stop by and spend a couple of nights with you so we can sip a few brews, and rehash our days in the old outfit.

"Then I'd sign it with a phony name, something like, 'Your old pal. Wilbur Crull." I was driving South on a sales trip the next week, so I took the cards along and mailed them from various small Southern towns.

"You can imagine how people reacted when the cards came. Wives were yelling, 'Who the hell is this guy? They're going to move in with us during Christmas?!!' Husbands were saying, 'For God's sake. I knew a hundred yokels in the Army. He could be any one of them!"

"My wife and I talked to several of them after they got the cards. They were in a panic. One couple had such an argument about his lousy old-time friends, they almost got divorced. Another friend of mine wouldn' answer his doorbell if he didn't recognize the person outside.

"You know what I'm going to do next Christmas?" I'm going to send them another card and say something like, 'Joe, old buddy. My pickup truck broke down, and we couldn't make it to Chicago last year. But we'll be there for sure this year, ya' hear?"

FLYING

"You've never been up in a plane?" a friend who was a pilot in the Air Force asked me back in 1947. "I'll sign out a training plane this Sunday and take you up."

What he didn't tell me was that he had agreed to be in an acrobatic air show. Instead of the gentle flight I was expecting, I found myself in the midst of loops, rolls, power dives, and all sorts of weird maneuvers.

"I blacked out three times on your power dives," I bitterly complained after we landed.

"So did I," he replied which didn't make me any happier about the experience.

"You didn't need to be afraid," a Presbyterian friend told me when I recounted the experience to him, "if it wasn't your time to go, the Lord wouldn't crash your plane."

Perhaps. But what happens if it's the pilot's time to go?

I've done a lot of flying since that time. But ever since that experience, I'm still not real comfortable with the whole thing. I find myself thinking as the plane goes rumbling down the runway, "There just ain't no way something this size can get off the ground."

I've decided that in order not to fear flying you either must be extremely intelligent, and fully understand aerodynamics, or else too stupid to comprehend anything about it. For example:

Two U. of Alabama graduates were flying from Alabama to London. Two hours into the flight, the captain announced:

"We've lost one engine, but it's no problem. We can fly on the remaining three. It'll just make us an hour late."

"We've lost another engine," he announced an hour later, "but we can make it okay with two engines. But rather than an hour it will make our arrival about two hours late."

"Gee," said one of the Alabama grads to his friend. "I hope we don't lose the other two engines. That would make us four hours late."

And I hate it when the captain talks to me on the loud speaker. First of all, I'm always on the left side of the plane when he says:

"If you'll look out the right window, you'll see a spectacular view of Banyan Canyon."

Secondly, he always times his announcemens just as I'm trying to take a nap and have just fallen asleep.

Thirdly, I want him paying attention to where he's steering this monstrosity, rather than serving as a tour guide.

"You don't need good distance vision to pilot a plane," a nearsighted pilot once told me. "You take off by instrument, fly by instrument, and do everything by instrument."

"But when you're coming down for a landing, how do you know when it's time to pull up the nose of the plane to keep from crashing?" I asked.

"Easy," he replied. "As soon as I hear the co-pilot scream, 'Aghhh!'"

THE LOTTERY

"Isn't it great that a poor person who really needs the money is the one who won all that money in the lottery?" I've often heard.

No, it is not!! First of all, it seems that in most such cases, they go hog wild and spend all the money, and end up worse off than they were. Or some sharpie adviser gets hold of them and ends up stealing all their money.

Even worse, it encourages other poor folks to waste the little money they have on buying lottery tickets, with almost no chance to win.

I do think it's good that lottery profits go to education scholarships. But as I heard one person describe it, "The lottery is a tax on poor people to send well to do peoples' kids to college."

TREATING SENIORS WITH CONDECENSCION

"What really gripes me is being called 'Nita' instead of 'Mrs. Read'," an 80 year old friend told me. "It's like they think older folks are in their second childhood, and treat us as if we are in our second childhood."

I'm a low key person, and really don't often get upset at what I'm called. But even I tend to become irritated, while sitting in a doctor's waiting room, to hear the teenage twerp receptionist call out in a tone of voice that suggested she felt she was addressing a six year old, "The doctor will see you now, Jack."

"I once caught a former receptionist of mine addressing an elderly patient who had just come to the window, 'Hi, Rose. Have a seat. Dr. London will see you in a few minutes," wrote Oscar London in his book, "Kill As Few Patients As Possible".

"Outraged, the patient said, 'How dare you call me Rose! Tell Oscar that Mrs. Schwartz decided to find another doctor.'"

"We don't get no respect," as Rodney Dangerfield says.

However I must admit that at times crotchety seniors act in ways in which they really don't deserve much respect. Like the retired elderly General, who had always been used to giving orders, and found it difficult not to continue doing so. Thus when he was in the hospital for surgery, he made a general nuisance of himself, ordering people around, and constantly complaining.

"It's time to take your temperature, General," said a male orderly. "Orders are that today we need to take it rectally." Griping all the while, the general finally turned over on his stomach, as the orderly inserted the thermometer.

"I'll be back in a few minutes," said the orderly as he left the room.

"What's all this about," said a nurse when she entered the room about five minutes later.

"Haven't you ever seen anyone have his temperature taken rectally," growled the general, sarcastically.

"Yes," she replied. "But never before with a daffodil."

LITTERING

I'm beginning to think that fast food restaurants put something in their food that makes temporary (or perhaps permanent) idiots out of folks. Surely otherwise there wouldn't be so many of them who toss bottles, cups, food containers, and other trash out of their car alongside the road. They can't wait until they get home to discard their trash, rather than littering the countryside?

Evidently however, it is not a stupidity limited to this country. A number of years ago while walking the streets of Paris, I noted that a lady walking ahead of me had inadvertently dropped her cigarette box. In the interest of demonstrating that Americans are gracious and thoughtful people, I picked up the box and rushed forward to return it to her. This however did little to foster good international relations. All I received for this good deed was an extremely dirty look from the lady. Only then did I discover the box was empty, and rather than dropping it, she had thrown it away.

SEEKING PERFECTION

"What's the most important thing you've learned in life?" was a survey question a few years ago. Many of the answers were thoughtful and serious, but some were lighthearted:
- Wherever you go, there you are.
- Eat your veggies.
- Make your own lunch

I particularly liked this one because it reminder me of a supposedly true story about former Cleveland Indians pitcher, Jim Bagby, who was evidently quite a character. He spent his off season from baseball working at the Lockheed Plant in Marietta, GA. A fellow worker there told of Bagby opening his lunch box at work one noon.

"Another peanut butter sandwich!" complained Bagby with disgust. "I hate peanut butter, and all I ever get is peanut butter sandwiches."

"Why don't you tell your wife what kind of sandwich you want, so that she'll quit fixing peanut butter sandwiches?"

"Wouldn't do any good," replied Bagby. "I fix my own damn lunch."

"You don't have to try to be number one in everything you do' would have been my answer," said the friend who told me of the survey. "I've found that life is easier if you're satisfied with second place. If you achieve second place you're still done well, and without as much stress."

I thought this was a great answer. And then I found this quote from a book by psychology professor Barry Schwartz:

"Maximizers are people who will accept only the best possible result, and never want to settle for second best. While this may sound like a good way to make choices, maximizers actually tend to be unhappy and dissatisfied with their lives."

Hence my dissatisfaction when I find myself trying to be a perfectionist.

But perhaps the best answer to the survey question about the most important thing he'd learned in life, came from the gentleman who said simply:

"Breathe!"

EFFICIENCY EXPERTS

"Why do you have a spoon in your shirt pocket?" asked the restaurant patron of the waiter.

"It's this damned new efficiency expert they've hired. If someone drops their spoon on the floor, we can give them the one in our pocket, saving the time of having to go all the way back to the kitchen."

"How about the string that's hanging out of your pants?"

"Same efficiency expert's idea. I'm supposed to use it when I go to the bathroom. That way I'm not touching anything, so I save the time I would have had to spend having to wash my hands."

"But how do you get it back in?"

"I don't know about the other waiters, but I use my spoon."

Made in the USA
Charleston, SC
14 December 2010